DATE DUE

Prisons

Today's Debate

Prisons
Today's Debate

Marilyn Tower Oliver

—Issues in Focus—

E **Enslow Publishers, Inc.**
44 Fadem Road   PO Box 38
Box 699   Aldershot
Springfield, NJ 07081   Hants GU12 6BP
USA   UK

To Lee and Pat Hancock, good friends, who always have fought for justice for all.

Library of Congress Cataloging-in-Publication Data

Oliver, Marilyn Tower.
    Prisons: today's debate / Marilyn Tower Oliver.
        p. cm. — (Issues in focus)
    Includes bibliographical references (p.   ) and index.
    Summary: Discusses problems relating to prisons, examines the controversy of whether prisons should rehabilitate or punish, and looks at possible alternatives to the current prison system.
    ISBN 0-89490-906-1
        1. Prisons—United States—Juvenile literature. 2. Prisoners—Rehabilitation—United States—Juvenile literature. 3. Alternatives to imprisonment—United States—Juvenile literature. [1. Prisons. 2. Prisoners.] I. Title. II. Series: Issues in focus (Hillside, N.J.)
HV9469.O55 1997
365'.973—dc21   96-40137
                                                              CIP
                                                              AC

Illustration Credits: California State Department of Corrections, pp. 11, 67, 70, 81, 103, 107; Library of Congress, pp. 19, 26, 30, 32, 54, 97; National Archives, pp. 40, 43, 76, 85, 92.

Cover Illustration: California State Department of Corrections

Contents

1

Prisons: A Problem for Society

In Detroit, Michigan, Damien Dorris, a fourteen-year-old drug dealer, and his accomplice, Jacob Gonzales, age ten, ambushed a pregnant mother of three after she withdrew eighty dollars from an automated teller machine. When she refused to hand over the money, Damien, who owed $430 to neighborhood drug kingpins, shot her in the head with a .22 caliber pistol. Jacob got twenty dollars of the take, which he spent to buy a chili dog and some toys.

When the boys were arrested the next day, Damien pleaded guilty to second-degree murder, and Jacob pleaded guilty to armed robbery. They were both given the maximum sentence—a prison term until each reaches the age of twenty-one. Jacob is serving his sentence in a children's home. Damien is confined in a maximum-security juvenile center. He had to spend five months in detention because there wasn't room for him in the more secure institution. It costs the state $200 a day to keep him locked up.[1]

7

■ ■ ■

In June 1996, Tony Hicks, a fifteen-year-old from San Diego, became the youngest person to be charged with murder in the state of California. Hicks used a 9-millimeter, semiautomatic handgun to shoot Tariq Khamisa, a twenty-year-old college student and pizza deliveryman. Khamisa had refused to give up the pizza or his cash.

Hicks was sentenced to twenty-five years to life in a California Youth Authority prison and will not be eligible for parole until he is thirty-six.

"I still don't know why I shot Tariq," he told the judge. "I didn't really want to hurt him. I'm sorry."[2]

■ ■ ■

Rising Crime Rates

Violent crimes committed by juveniles under eighteen have increased during the last decades of the twentieth century. In 1991 the number of young people arrested was 5.6 percent higher than in 1982.[3]

Adult crime is also a serious problem. Convicted criminals are crowding the nation's prisons. By the end of 1995, the total number of prisoners under state or federal control was 1,585,400, compared to 329,821 in 1980. This equals 600 inmates for every 100,000 residents of the United States. The states with the highest number of prisoners were California, Texas, and New York. Prisons were seriously overcrowded. State prison systems were operating between 14 and 25 percent over capacity, and federal prisons operated at 26 percent over capacity.[4]

A higher number of drug convictions is one reason for the rising number of prisoners. The percentage of

8

state prisoners serving a drug sentence more than tripled from 1980 to 1993.

Alarmed by what they see as a high crime rate, many citizens are demanding more prisons and longer sentences. Unfortunately, prison construction has not kept up with the growing number of convicted prisoners.

Many people also want prisons to be harsh and uncomfortable. They complain that prisons are often too permissive rather than being strict places of punishment. They point to examples such as these:

- Thirty-three convicts, mostly murderers, serving life sentences at the Correctional Institution in Norfolk, Massachusetts, and forty-nine of their guests enjoyed a catered prime-rib dinner at their annual "Lifers' Banquet."

- At high-security Sullivan Prison in Fallsburg, New York, inmates exercise in an outdoor area that is outfitted with barbells and other exercise equipment. While they work out, they can watch their favorite television shows on outdoor television sets. A music room at the same prison allows prisoners to practice on electric guitars, keyboards, and drums.

- In a Missouri prison, an inmate-run closed-circuit television station broadcasts movies filled with violence and sex.

On the other side, those who support prison reform believe that education and recreation help train prisoners to reenter society as useful citizens.

Critics of current prison policies, however, point to statistics that show that a high percentage of convicts return to crime after they are released. According to the

9

U.S. Bureau of Justice Statistics, as many as 60 to 70 percent of inmates return to a life of crime after release.[5]

Take the example of Conrad Jeffrey. Jeffrey was arrested in 1985 for the kidnapping and attempted sexual assault of a twelve-year-old boy in New Jersey. Through plea bargaining, the charges were reduced to kidnapping. Plea bargaining is a process in which an accused person confesses to a lesser crime to receive a shorter sentence rather than make the government pay for a trial. Jeffrey was sentenced to five years in prison. He got out in less than two years.

Out of prison, Jeffrey returned to a life of crime and was caught. He was sentenced to serve four years in prison, but again he was paroled. Back in society, he pulled a knife on a teenage girl and was sentenced to serve two and a half years. When he finished serving that term, he committed a much more serious crime. He was accused of kidnapping and murdering a seven-year-old girl.[6]

In recent years, citizens in many states have demanded tougher sentencing laws such as three-strikes laws and mandatory minimum sentences. Three-strikes laws require sending an individual to prison for a long term, perhaps for life, after he or she is convicted of a third felony. A felony is a serious crime such as murder, rape, or armed robbery. Mandatory minimum sentences require a judge to sentence a convicted person to serve a specific number of years depending on the crime he or she has committed. In 1996 three-strikes laws were on the books in twenty-four states.[7]

Are these tough measures a good way to control crime? What role does rehabilitation play? Some

Prisoners in this California prison are housed in a multitiered cellblock.

criminologists point out that most prisoners will someday rejoin society. They say that these people need education, job training, and counseling to help them become law-abiding citizens upon release.

There are many reasons why people commit crimes. Studies show that children who have been abused or neglected are more likely to be arrested for violent crimes.[8]

A greater percentage of African Americans and Latinos than whites are in prison. In December 1993, nearly two thirds of all sentenced prison inmates were black, Asian, Native American, or Hispanic. Many of these individuals are poor.

Critics of the prison system say that the law does not treat everyone in an equal manner. They say that lawbreakers who are wealthy can buy a better defense and are less likely to end up in prison to serve long sentences than are those who are poor.

Arguments about the treatment of prisoners are not new. Should prisons be places where criminals are punished, perhaps harshly, for their crimes, or should the role of prisons be to educate and reform offenders to become better citizens? Looking at the way prisoners have been treated in the past will better help us understand the problems facing prisons today.

2

Prisons in the Western World

In the past, prisons were harsh and often cruel places where lawbreakers were kept until the authorities decided what to do with them. The usual punishments were torture, exile, or execution. In addition to those who committed crimes such as murder and stealing, people could be imprisoned for owing money or for holding different religious or political beliefs. Justice was swift, and lawbreakers were not usually kept in prison for long periods of time as many are today.

In the earliest societies, the tribe or social group determined which behaviors were acceptable and which were not. Murder, rape, and kidnapping were not always considered crimes, but they might lead to a blood feud between clans or families. The leaders of the tribe only got involved when the feud threatened the society as a whole. Other forbidden behaviors, sometimes called taboos, were actions that hurt the tribe. For example,

13

among the Plains nations in North America, it was illegal to scare away the buffalo.[1]

The development of writing was soon followed by written laws that spelled out punishments for specific crimes. Some of the punishments were execution, mutilation, and exile.

While cultures all over the world have developed ways to punish those who break laws, our systems of punishment come from the traditions of western culture.

Prisons in the Ancient World

Courts in ancient Greece often sentenced offenders to repay their victims. Community service such as building roads was another popular sentence. Those who committed serious crimes were killed or exiled.[2]

In 450 B.C., the Greeks built a prison in Athens to hold criminals sentenced to death. The condemned person was forced to commit suicide by drinking a poison called hemlock. The most famous prisoner sentenced to die in this prison was the philosopher Socrates, who drank hemlock in 399 B.C.[3] Socrates was condemned to this painful death because the authorities believed that he was corrupting his young followers by teaching them to question religion.

In ancient Rome, prisoners were held until the authorities decided whether they should be punished or set free.[4]

In the Middle Ages the Catholic Church Controlled Prisoners

During the Middle Ages, religion played a large part in the punishment of wrongdoers. To maintain order, the Catholic Church built prisons as places to keep offenders.

14

One of the most serious crimes was heresy. Heresy is expressing opinions that are in opposition to church teaching. A person convicted of heresy might be expelled from the church. In some cases, the offender might be condemned to death by burning at the stake. The church courts also handled other crimes such as rape, burglary, and homicide. The belief that prisoners could be rehabilitated or reformed was developed by the Roman Catholics. The last Catholic prison was built in Paris in the sixteenth century.

Prisons and Penalties in England

English law was based on Anglo-Saxon rather than Roman traditions. Imprisonment for committing a crime was more common in England than in the rest of Europe.

Newgate, one of London's oldest prisons, was probably built around 1190. Prisoners who had been condemned to death were kept in the hold, a small, dark room near the gate of the prison. New prisoners were also kept in the hold until they could pay to be moved to one of two sections of the prison. More wealthy prisoners paid to be sent to the Master's Side, a part of the prison where conditions were not as harsh. They could pay for such extras as a fire during the cold winter months, a bed, and the privilege of having visitors, who also had to pay when they visited.

Those who could not afford to pay were sent to the Common Side, a miserable area that had an underground dungeon called the Stone Hold. Here, prisoners had no beds and slept on the stone floor. A part of the prison called the Middle Ward was for prisoners who could pay

15

only the basic fee. Although beds were not furnished, the prisoners slept on wooden floors.[5]

Most sixteenth-century prisons were still places where criminals could be safely held until judgment. Some were also places for correction.

At this time, many people were moving from the countryside to the cities to find work. Before the sixteenth century, many people had farmed land for a noble or lord in exchange for protection. When this system, called feudalism, broke down, the workers were forced to leave the land. Unable to find employment in the cities, many became homeless. Just being without a home and a job was considered a crime. Vagrants, people who wandered about without jobs, were punished by whipping. They were also thrown into prison to wait for trial.

In 1597 the Act for the Punishment of Rogues, Vagabonds, and Sturdy Beggars required that such people were to be kept in a jail or prison until they could be put to work. They still might receive a whipping. Those who were not so easily reformed were to be sent to the undeveloped lands under British rule: the American colonies and Australia.

Like prisons, jails were horrible places, and many prisoners died before they could come to trial. Some jails were in the cellars of old castles or in county courthouses. Others were back rooms in inns or taverns.

Debtors, people who owed money, were also placed in prison. Because they were poor, they were often treated more harshly than criminals who could pay for better living conditions. Men and women were kept together. Murderers and the homeless were often imprisoned side by side.[6]

In 1533 King Henry VI turned over a former royal palace in London to be used as a workhouse for the poor. This house of correction was named Bridewell. Prisoners were taught skills such as spinning cloth or baking bread.

After 1576 a new law created similar workhouses in other parts of England. These prisons for the homeless all came to be called Bridewells. Although they were designed to help those who were unemployed and homeless, they soon became crowded and badly run. In addition to the homeless, orphans, runaways, and the mentally ill filled the workhouses.[7] As bad as they were, the workhouses set a precedent for rehabilitation in prison that still exists today.

Other parts of Europe were influenced by the British workhouses. In the Netherlands a spinning house for women was founded in 1596. In Rome Pope Clement XI founded the Hospice of San Michele, a reformatory for boys. A hospice was a place of refuge. The goal of the reformatory was to teach unruly boys to pray, to work, and to regret their bad behavior. Boys were classified according to their ages and to the seriousness of their crimes. Each prisoner worked during the day and at night was placed in an individual cell. In 1735 Clement opened a similar reformatory for women.

The most revolutionary of the workhouses was the House of Correction in Ghent, Belgium, founded in the early 1770s. At this prison, women and children were separated from the men. Prisoners were taught trades as a form of rehabilitation.[8]

Although there were efforts at prison reform, most prisoners were kept until they could be punished. Punishment in the eighteenth century was cruel, and mutilation and death were common. Those found guilty of lesser offenses, called misdemeanors, were often whipped. In England, men, and even women, were tied to the back of a cart and whipped as they were forced to run through the streets. If the crime caused public anger, a collection might be taken to give to the man who was to do the whipping, to encourage him to beat the prisoner more harshly.

Some prisoners were sentenced to the pillory or the stocks. The pillory was a device that held the victim's head and hands. The stocks held the feet or feet and hands. The public would be allowed to torment unpopular prisoners by throwing stones or rotten fish and vegetables at them. Sometimes the prisoners' clothes were torn from their bodies. By the nineteenth century, the use of the pillory and the stocks was dying out.

Women prisoners were not spared harsh punishments. The public could sometimes get permission to witness the whipping of prostitutes in Bridewell. The prostitute would be sentenced to be whipped until her back was bloody. In 1820 the whipping of women was abolished.[9]

Executions

Execution was the punishment for many offenses. Serious crimes such as treason, murder, arson, and rape were not the only offenses punished by death. Less serious crimes such as cutting down trees without permission and hiding some possessions when declaring bankruptcy could also lead to a death sentence. Executions were held in public because it was believed that watching the

18

In the past, placing prisoners in stocks was a common punishment. This punishment was used during the nineteenth century in the United States.

prisoners die would discourage crime. Hanging days were unofficial holidays, and people flocked to see public executions, which might be held eight times a year in London.

On a hanging day, church bells rang muffled. The prisoners were taken to the place of execution in an open cart. Crowds along the way would cheer popular figures such as highwaymen. In the eighteenth century, highwaymen who robbed travellers sometimes were seen as glamorous and daring figures. On the other hand, if a condemned prisoner had committed a murder that caused public anger, people would jeer and throw things at him. The carts were stopped at taverns along the way where the prisoners would be served jugs of ale. Sometimes criminals were hanged at the scene of their crime, on a portable gallows.

Although most criminals were hanged, some suffered a more terrible death. Most of those convicted of treason, attempting to overthrow or undermine the government, were hanged, drawn, and quartered. The prisoner would be cut from the gallows before he died. Then, the executioner would cut out the prisoner's bowels, and his body was hacked into four pieces.

Women who were guilty of treason were burned alive. A woman who killed her husband would be tied to a tall stake or pole and then burned. Sometimes she would be hanged from an iron ring at the top of the stake, and a fire would be set at her feet. In the early eighteenth century, the executioner would strangle the woman before she was burned. In 1753 a woman named Anne Williams was the last woman to be burned for killing her husband.[10]

Exile as Punishment

Forcing a prisoner to leave England was an alternative to the death penalty. Between 1732 and 1776, an estimated 50,000 to 100,000 English convicts were sent to the American colonies.[11]

Elizabeth Sprigs was a young female prisoner who was sent to Maryland. In 1756, in a letter to her father, she described her life as a servant in the New World. She wrote that she was forced to work day and night and was often tied up and whipped. Her diet consisted of corn and salt.[12]

After the American Revolution some prisoners were sent from England to Australia, then an undeveloped, wild country. Others were placed in prison ships that floated on the River Thames. John Wade, a journalist and historian writing in 1829, described the prison ships. One ship, the *Euryalus*, was for boys sixteen years of age and younger. They were taught shoemaking, tailoring, and bookbinding. When prisoners arrived at the prison ships, they were stripped and dressed in prison clothes. Iron shackles were placed on one of the prisoner's legs. The boys' diet consisted of oatmeal, barley, bread, beef, cheese, salt, and beer.[13]

Reforms

In the late eighteenth century, some people became concerned about the harsh and inhumane treatment of prisoners in England. John Howard was a reformer who was shocked by the conditions of prisoners. In 1773, after visiting English prisons, he began a campaign for reform. In one prison he had found prisoners chained to the floor to keep them from escaping. Each prisoner had to wear an iron collar around his neck. The collar had twelve-inch spikes that kept him from moving. Other prisons were rat infested. Prisoners were often half-starved.[14]

In 1777 Howard wrote a book, *The State of Prisons in England and Wales.* Among the reforms he championed were individual cells for prisoners and adequate food and medical care. He called for a program of silence and solitary confinement to encourage the prisoners to be sorry for their crimes. He called the new prisons penitentiaries because they encouraged the prisoners to be penitent, or to regret their past actions.

In 1779 Howard encouraged Parliament to pass the Penitentiary Act. This act called for building penitentiaries with individual cells and prison inspections. Prisoners would not have to pay for services in prisons. Howard was appointed to oversee the construction of the new prisons. When arguing broke out about where they should be built, he resigned. Twelve years passed before Parliament reconsidered the prison problem.[15]

Prisons in America

In colonial America, sentencing a criminal to prison was even rarer than in Europe, because there was a shortage of men to serve as guards. The strong and able-bodied were needed to work in the colonies. The prisons that did exist followed the pattern set in England. Treatment of prisoners was also harsh and cruel.

One group, the Quakers, had an important role in creating prisons in the New World. Quakers are a religious sect or group that believes in nonviolence. This group, who settled in New Jersey and Pennsylvania, rejected the death penalty and punishments such as whipping. They believed that a prisoner could be reformed through hard work and time to think about his or her wrongdoing.

In 1787 Quakers and other humanitarians under the leadership of Dr. Benjamin Rush formed the Philadelphia Society for Alleviating the Miseries of Public Prisons. This group, now known as the Pennsylvania Prison Society, is the oldest prison reform group in the United States.

They encouraged the Pennsylvania legislature to build a model penitentiary in the Walnut Street Jail in Philadelphia. The hope was that treatment of the prisoners would encourage rehabilitation so they could reenter society. The system developed in Pennsylvania came to be known as the silent system.

Prisoners were to be given a sentence of a specific length of time, called a determinate sentence, which could not be shortened by good behavior. Those who had committed violent crimes were separated from less violent prisoners.

Hardened prisoners lived in solitary confinement so that they could reflect on their crimes and study the Bible. They also worked in their cells. Each cell had a small exercise yard. The prisoners were not allowed to mingle with one another. For its time, the Pennsylvania system was considered humane.

In 1818 two huge penitentiaries were ordered built by the Pennsylvania legislature. Western Penitentiary was built in Pittsburgh. Eastern Penitentiary, called Cherry Hill because it was built on the site of a cherry orchard, was in Philadelphia. At this prison, inmates were kept in strict solitary confinement. They were blindfolded when they entered the prison, and while serving their sentence, they worked, slept, and ate alone.

In New York, a harsher approach was followed. At Auburn State Prison, founded in 1815, prisoners were allowed to work in groups, but they could not speak to one another. This came to be known as the congregate system. To congregate means to gather or meet together. When they weren't working, prisoners had to stay in their tiny cells. Many states followed the Auburn system because it was more economical.[16]

The idea that prisoners could not communicate with one another led to severe discipline problems. Some reformers believed that enforced silence was very cruel. Forced silence and solitary confinement were said to cause many prisoners to become insane.[17]

The strict silence and hard work did not seem to lead to rehabilitation. The determinate sentence meant that prisoners had to spend a determined number of years in prison even if they behaved well. There wasn't an incentive to improve. Prison officials also viewed prisoners' work as a way to bring money to the prisons. Guards sometimes used cruel methods to make prisoners work harder.

Both the silent system of prisons used in Pennsylvania and the congregate or group system of New York had critics. Some said that the loneliness of the solitary confinement practiced in Pennsylvania prisons caused some inmates to go insane. They argued that this was cruel. Others criticized the congregate approach of the New York prisons because it seemed cruel to allow prisoners to work together without allowing them to communicate. This was also hard to enforce.

Then, as today, there was much disagreement as to whether the main purpose of prisons was rehabilitation or punishment.

Prisons in the South

Not all states had penitentiaries in the early part of the nineteenth century.

In some of the southern states, many people thought that penitentiaries violated individual rights. They believed that it was more humane to punish a wrongdoer and allow him to return to his family. Branding and whipping were among the punishments used.

Supporters of building penitentiaries ranged between 3 percent to 30 percent of the population. Most were more highly educated than the general population. Eventually their ideas won out. Before the Civil War, most of the state legislatures had voted to build penitentiaries.[18]

Once established, the routine of the southern prisons was similar to that of prisons in the North. The inmates' day was spent at work and in silence. At dawn, prisoners were awakened by a loud trumpet. Cell doors were opened, and prisoners stepped out, closing the doors behind them. Then they marched to workbenches where they would labor without speaking until breakfast. Prisoners worked six days a week from sunrise to sunset. On Sunday, they would hear sermons and walk in the yard. If they had behaved during the week, they would be rewarded with tobacco to chew.

Prisoners often rebelled against this strict routine. Inmates sometimes set fires or started fights. In 1860 forty

Convict labor was popular in the South. Prisoners were expected to
pay their own way, and if possible, make money for the state.

prisoners revolted at Mississippi's prison textile factory. In the fighting one convict was killed, and six were wounded.

Before the Civil War, most southern prisoners were poor white men. Slaves were punished by their owners rather than going to prison. The few African Americans in the South who went to prison were freemen. In the 1850s these made up only one percent of the prison population in Mississippi and Alabama and only 4 percent of the prisoners in Tennessee. However, in Virginia a third of the prisoners were African-American.

Women in southern prisons suffered much abuse. They were considered too wicked to be worthy of concern. Because cells were not built for them, they were kept in dirty buildings inside the prison grounds.[19]

Prisons were expected to support themselves, and if possible, add to the state treasury. Work became a way of life in many penitentiaries. In the 1850s, Georgia convicts built 371 railroad cars for the state-owned railroad. In Mississippi the state built a prison cotton factory in 1849. The cloth produced by this factory brought the state a $20,000-a-year profit. Because most prison business did not make money, officials began to lease convicts to businesspeople.[20]

The Movement for Change

Prison reformers realized that the harsh methods were not producing fewer prisoners. In 1850 there were approximately seven thousand prisoners in America; by 1870 there were thirty-three thousand.[21]

In the 1830s in Ireland, Richard Whately, the Archbishop of Dublin, urged releasing back to the community prisoners who had records of good behavior. This

27

idea interested those who wanted to reform American prisons.

They were also influenced by the methods of Captain Alexander Maconochie, the administrator of a harsh prison colony on Norfolk Island in Australia. Maconochie made up a system in which inmates could reduce their sentences through good conduct. Upon release, inmates could return to England. He was considered a radical and was fired in 1849, but his ideas were important in changing the way prisoners were treated in Ireland and later in the United States.[22]

In the United States, prison officials were considering reforms. In 1867 Michigan was the first state to legislate the indeterminate sentence, largely due to the efforts of Zebulon R. Brockway, superintendent of the Detroit House of Correction. With an indeterminate sentence, a prisoner can shorten the length of time in prison through good behavior.

In 1870, a group of prison officials met in Cincinnati, Ohio, to discuss reform in the penitentiaries. A result of this meeting was the birth of the American Correctional Association, an organization of professional prison administrators and penologists, people who are interested in prison reform and management.

The members of the American Correctional Association believed that prisoners, especially young offenders, needed special attention. Vocational education was a priority.

In 1876, the state of New York opened Elmira Reformatory, a prison for young offenders between the ages of sixteen and thirty. A portion of the prisoner's earnings was set aside for him to use after he was released.

28

There was an attempt at rehabilitation. Inmates were to receive an education that included physical and military training. Prisoners at Elmira also had a library, a glee club, an athletic field, and a gym. Prisoners were given indeterminate sentences, which could be shortened with good behavior. After prisoners were released, they were supervised by special agents. These agents were the first probation officers. Many of the principles of the new institution are still in effect today.[23]

Prison officials were confident that the new ideas would succeed, but by 1900 it was evident that there were problems.

Lack of money was partly responsible. The new reforms were expensive. The indeterminate sentence was also to blame. Offenders learned how to beat the system by doing the things that would get the parole boards to release them.

The reformatories, however, did bring about changes in the ways prisoners are treated today.[24] Separating young prisoners from older, hardened criminals was one policy that has continued. Women prisoners are now housed separately from men. It was also learned that not all prisoners should be treated alike. Today's minimum-, medium-, and maximum-security prisons are a result.

New Theories Make Changes

In the nineteenth and early twentieth centuries, at the same time politicians and prison officials were arguing about the treatment of prisoners in America, new theories about man and his actions were being developed. Author and scholar Charles Darwin wrote about his theory of

At Elmira State Reformatory, opened in 1876 in New York, young
offenders between the ages of sixteen and thirty lived by strict rules.
Here, they are lined up for a dress parade.

evolution, which held that man had evolved or developed from simpler forms of life. Sigmund Freud, an Austrian psychologist, studied mental illness and developed a theory that human behavior was based on the way a person was treated as a child. These theories were to affect the way prisoners would be treated.

In 1889 Cesare Lombroso, an Italian doctor, published *The Criminal Man.* Lombroso's theories suggested that criminals were a throwback to primitive man. He argued that there was a connection between a person's physical characteristics and the likelihood that he would become a criminal. A person with a small nose, receding forehead, and thin beard was likely to become a robber. A murderer might have glassy eyes and a nose like a hawk. His theories were based on physical studies he made of lawbreakers. Although his beliefs are discredited today, he is remembered because he tried to use scientific methods of observation to study criminality to explain why people committed crimes. An earlier theory held that a criminal was born with the tendency to commit crimes.[25] Psychologists who came along after Lombroso have studied prisoners' lives to try to explain their behavior.

Psychology also led to new ways of treating prisoners. Some psychologists believed that criminals broke laws because they were mentally ill. Prisoners were tested and interviewed to determine the causes for their behavior. Treatments, called therapy, were designed to help cure their illness. Prisoners were encouraged to talk their problems over with psychologists and in group sessions. Although therapy is still used in some prisons, the method was particularly popular from the 1930s to the early 1970s.[26]

Although the psychological approach to corrections

31

In the nineteenth and early twentieth centuries, people accused of a crime were judged in a courtroom where the judge and all the jury were men.

helped some prisoners, it also led to problems. Prisoners learned to tell the psychologists and the parole boards that they had come to grips with their psychological problems in the hopes of getting an early release.

"The saying among inmates is 'get a program.' They know it helps with the parole board," said criminologist Charles Logan of the University of Connecticut. "Despite claims to the contrary, no type of treatment has been effective in rehabilitating criminals or preventing future criminal behavior."[27]

In the 1970s and 1980s, concern over the prison conditions led to new reforms. Prisoners were allowed to receive uncensored mail. Because many inmates were from minority groups, guards were recruited from those groups. Drug rehabilitation was offered to help prisoners kick their habits. Inmates were encouraged to complete their education and get job training.

Unfortunately, like reforms of the past, these changes did not reduce the arrest rate. The number of inmates in the United States has continued to climb. This is partly due to the war on drugs, which has resulted in greatly increasing the number of inmates in the nation's prisons.

Another reason is public concern about crime, which has led citizens to demand more convictions and longer prison sentences. More arrests lead to overcrowded prisons. To create room, some inmates are released after they have served only a part of their sentences. Many of these return to a life of crime, and the cycle continues.

Clearly, crime and punishment are complex problems.

3

Prison Systems

The correctional system of the United States is made up of different jurisdictions or authorities. After being arrested, a person may be held in a local or county jail. Local jails, also called lockups, usually hold people who are accused of a crime and are awaiting trial.

County prisons house offenders who have been convicted of lesser crimes, called misdemeanors. If the state prison system is highly overcrowded, some felons, found guilty of more serious crimes, may also serve time in a county facility.

Inmates in federal and state prisons may have committed crimes such as murder, armed robbery, or rape. Those found guilty of other crimes such as drug trafficking or embezzlement (which is stealing funds belonging to a business or an organization) may also be housed in a state or federal prison. Federal prisons incarcerate those

35

who have been convicted of breaking federal laws. State prisoners have been found guilty of breaking state laws.

The people in prisons and jails are not the only ones caught up in the correctional system. The system also includes people out on bail and waiting to go to trial. Bail is an amount of money an arrested person deposits with the court to guarantee that he or she will return for trial.

Inmates released on parole, and people who have received probation are also a part of the system. Parole is granted to prisoners who have served part of their sentences and have earned release through good behavior. Probation substitutes for a prison term. The person on probation must avoid criminal associations and lead a crime-free life. He or she has to meet with a probation officer, who monitors the person's behavior. If a person fails to live up to the rules of probation, it can be canceled, and the person will start to serve a prison term.

The Federal Prison

Although individual states had prisons as early as 1790, the federal prison system was not formed until one hundred years later.

In 1891 Congress passed legislation to establish three federal penitentiaries. These were at Leavenworth, Kansas; in Atlanta, Georgia; and on McNeil's Island, off the coast of Washington State. The prisons were designed to house criminals who were found guilty of the most serious crimes such as murder, kidnapping, or treason. They were prisons for men. Because women also commit serious crimes, the Federal Reformatory for Women opened in West Virginia in 1925.

36

Alcatraz, perhaps America's most famous prison, had a high degree of security because it was surrounded by the water of San Francisco Bay. From 1933 to 1973, this federal prison housed some of the nation's most dangerous criminals. It was closed in 1973.

In the first few decades of the twentieth century, criminal activity began to increase. This was due mostly to two factors.

The first factor was Prohibition. In 1920 the Eighteenth Amendment to the Constitution made it illegal to manufacture, sell, or transport alcoholic beverages in the United States. The law was in effect for thirteen years and was repealed by the Twenty-first Amendment in 1933.

Prohibition led to the formation of two new government agencies. The Federal Bureau of Investigation (FBI) was created by reorganizing the Bureau of Investigation, a part of the United States Justice Department. The new agency was to investigate crimes such as spying, kidnapping, government fraud, and transporting illegal property across state lines. In 1930 Congress established the Bureau of Prisons, also a part of the Justice Department. This bureau manages the federal prison system.

Prohibition had the result of causing more crime punishable at the federal level. The new law did not abolish liquor, but it made the sale of alcoholic beverages illegal. To get around the law, a new group of criminals, called bootleggers, smuggled and sold liquor in violation of federal laws.

A second factor in the increase of crime in the early twentieth century was the new popularity of the automobile. In the early 1900s cars were rare. By the 1920s they

37

had become common. More cars on the road led to a new crime—auto theft. Soon, Congress made it a federal offense to take a stolen car across state lines. The increase in crime lead to the construction of more federal prisons to house convicted car thieves and bootleggers.

Today, the federal prison system has its headquarters in Washington, D.C. The system is made up of men's and women's prisons and prisons for juvenile offenders. Criminals who are convicted of crimes that cross state lines may end up in a federal prison. The chief official in a federal prison, called the warden or superintendent, oversees the administration of the prison. The guards or correctional officers, who make up one third to one half of all the employees in the Bureau of Prisons, are responsible for keeping order. In the prisons, there are also social workers, teachers, psychologists, doctors, and nurses.[1]

McKean, a model federal correctional institution in Bradford, Pennsylvania, is a very modern prison. A medium-security prison, McKean is a cluster of low buildings surrounded by well-tended lawns and athletic fields. The prison offers inmates classes in reading, masonry, carpentry, barbering, and catering. Forty-seven percent of the inmates are enrolled in classes, one of the highest rates in the federal system. The prison costs the taxpayers approximately $15,370 a year for each inmate, a cost that is below the overall federal average of $21,350.[2]

State Prisons

The United States is made up of fifty states, and each state has a prison system to house felons who have broken state laws. Some inmates serving time in state prisons have committed very serious crimes such as murder, rape, and armed robbery. Inmates who have committed less violent crimes such as forgery might also serve time in a state prison. Usually, a prisoner is held in the state where he has committed the offense. Prison systems vary from state to state.

The earliest state prison was Walnut Street Jail in Philadelphia, built in 1790. Most of the early prisons were in the North because these states had larger populations. By the beginning of the Civil War in 1861, most of southern states had also built penitentiaries patterned on those in the North. After the Civil War ended with the defeat of the Confederacy in 1865, the South was in chaos. Much of the farmland and many of the cities had been destroyed in the fighting. Prison reform was not a priority. Because many people opposed paying for the care of prisoners, inmates were expected to work to support the prisons and to bring money to the state treasury. This practice was not new. In Texas, prisoners had been expected to pay their own way as early as 1849, when the state built its first prison at Huntsville.

After slavery was abolished in 1865, southern prisoners worked to build railroads, river canals, and other public utilities. Their wages went to pay for prison expenses. In 1871 in Texas, the court case *Ruffin* v. *Commonwealth* certified inmates as servants of the state.[3]

In some southern states, prisoners were also forced to work in chain gangs. The prisoners, wearing leg-irons, were chained together and taken out to build roads and bridges and to clear brush. Often they were forced to work for twelve hours at a time. Guards with whips and guns made sure that order was kept.

39

This prison in Tallahassee, Florida, is typical of many state prisons. Barbed wire surrounds the compound of secure buildings to make sure no one escapes.

"It kept men out of doors in God's open country . . . where they could enjoy the singing of birds," said one southern senator in defense of the practice in the late 1930s.[4]

In the nineteenth century, prison officials found that even with the prison industries, prisoners were not paying their way. To resolve this problem, prisoners were often contracted out to private companies or individuals as workers. This practice reduced the cost the state had to pay to care for prisoners. However, the system was often brutal, and prisoners were treated cruelly. Punishments for misbehavior included confinement in irons, and prisoners were sometimes whipped. Some were punished on a cruel device called the horse. It was a vertical post that had slots into which a peg was fitted. The prisoner was forced to sit with his back against the post. His hands were tied behind him, and his feet were brought down tightly and stretched with great tension. Prisoners were also kicked and beaten. The stocks were often used.

The desire to cut costs also had other consequences. As with today, overcrowding was a serious problem. By 1873, Huntsville Prison in Texas had 676 convicts housed in 278 cells. On average, three convicts had to share a small cell that was seven feet two inches high, five feet wide, and seven feet long. Thirteen inmates were under fourteen years of age, and some were as young as nine.[5]

In the North, some prisons were turned into factories in which convict labor was used to make products for private manufacturers. Although prisoners were paid a small sum for their work, prison conditions continued to be harsh. When unemployment was high, people complained that prisoners were working while law-abiding citizens could not find work. They argued that products made by convicts for low wages would compete with those produced outside prison.[6]

Prisons Differ from State to State

Today, after a person is convicted of a crime, he or she usually serves time in the state where the crime was committed. Prisons differ from state to state and from place to place.

The state prison system in California is the nation's largest. Like most state systems, it has three main objectives. It asks that inmates be accountable for their crimes, that they be productive while in prison, and that they leave with tools to succeed as nonoffenders. The system operates three licensed hospitals. Each prison has an infirmary and a dental clinic. Chaplains attend to the prisoners' spiritual needs. Teachers help inmates prepare for a life outside prison walls. Above all these considerations, however, is the need to keep the prisons secure and escape-free.

In California, as in other states, prisons range from minimum to maximum security. Minimum-security prisons usually do not have fences. Inmates may be housed in dormitories rather than in cells. Inmates serving longer sentences and who have prior records may go to a medium-security prison, where they are housed in cells. The boundaries of the prison are fenced, and armed guards keep order. The most violent prisoners are housed in maximum-security prisons. In addition to cells and fenced or walled boundaries, security is enforced by more armed guards and electronic devices.[7]

In the northern states, prison factories used convict workers to make goods for manufacturers. These convicts in a Connecticut prison worked at making gloves.

Life in most state prisons in the United States is tedious at best and harsh and dangerous at worst. Many prisons are overcrowded. When prisoners are forced to live in crowded situations, the possibility of violence is greater.

At the end of 1994, California prisons were operating at 184 percent of their capacity. The New Jersey prison system was at 142 percent of its capacity. Illinois prisons were at 138 percent of the planned capacity. Nationwide, state prisons were estimated to be housing more prisoners than they were designed to hold.[8]

Crowding leads to violence and the need to build even more secure prisons.

California has built a high-security prison called Pelican Bay State Penitentiary in the northern part of the state to house the most dangerous prisoners who have caused problems in other prisons. These prisoners have started serious fights or have been involved in prison gangs. This prison is stark and fortresslike. Prisoners are chained as they travel from their cells to the library. Prisoners receive their food trays through a slot in their cell door. They are stripped and body searched whenever they leave their cells.[9]

In the 1990s, several states brought back the chain gang as a form of punishment for prisoners. This controversial practice has both critics and defenders. In 1996, at Limestone Correctional Facility in Athens, Alabama, 400 convicts worked in squads of 40. The prisoners wore white uniforms and were chained together, ankle to ankle, in groups of five. Chain gangs are less expensive for the state because one officer can guard forty chained prisoners. Without chains, an officer can only guard twenty convicts.

Florida and Arizona also have chain gangs; other states have considered them. They appeal to voters who demand that prisoners be punished rather than rehabilitated.

What does it feel like to be on a chain gang?

"I see now how that dog on a chain feels. Mentally, it's worse than anything. You got to have one on your leg to know what I'm talking about," one inmate, a thief who was arrested for stealing a bag of clothes, said.[10]

City and County Jails and Prisons

When state and federal prisons cannot hold all the convicted lawbreakers, some must serve their time in another place such as a county prison. Usually, these inmates have been sentenced to a shorter term of a year or less.

Jails are temporary holding sites for people who have been arrested and who are waiting for trial. At the federal level, a jail is called a detention center.

"Compared to state and federal prisons, local lockups are unglamorous, underfunded and unnoticed, yet they hold nearly a third of all the prisoners in the country," says an article in *The Angolite*, a bimonthly magazine published by inmates at Angola State Prison in Louisiana.

According to a federal Bureau of Justice Statistics census of jails at mid-year 1994, close to a half million people were locked up in American jails. These include many state and federal inmates for whom there is no room in the penitentiary. In Louisiana there were nine thousand state prisoners serving time in local lockups. This was a rate of 377 prisoners for every 100,000 people in the state.[11]

As in state and federal prisons, large urban jails and detention centers are often overcrowded, and violence often breaks out.

New York's Rikers Island jail holds city and state parole violators, those waiting for trial, sex offenders, runaways, sentenced drug addicts, and those who are accused of serious crimes such as murder. Rikers has six jails exclusively for men. One of these is a high-security jail where dangerous inmates are guarded. In addition, there are four special units. One is for women, one for convicted and sentenced men, and two are for prisoners who have special medical needs. There are approximately fifteen thousand inmates in Rikers Island.[12]

Prison gangs challenge the system at Rikers. As of 1994, the Department of Correction has identified at least twelve hundred gang members. Because the groups recruit members in the other city jails, the number may actually be higher. The gang members use hand signals to communicate with one another in defiance of guards.[13]

In Los Angeles County, many dangerous criminals are held in jail dormitories that were never meant to house vicious felons. Los Angeles County, which contains eight major facilities, makes up the nation's largest jail system. Each year it handles 250,000 prisoners. At any one time, 18,000 to 20,000 men and women are locked up to wait for trial, to serve sentences, or to wait for transit to and from the courts and the state prisons.

At Pitchess Detention Center, a Los Angeles County prison, gang fights and race riots are a common occurrence. The fights and race riots are masterminded by tattooed gang leaders called "shot-callers."[14]

Local facilities often have less control over inmates'

behavior than do state prisons. In the state system, gangs can be broken up by moving prisoners to different prisons. In some jails where inmates live close together in dormitories, there is more opportunity for gang violence to break out.

In addition to prisons and jails, there are other places where a person may be detained. After being arrested, a person may spend time in a police station lockup. Other prisoners just about to be released may be kept in a pre-release center.

Bail

Not everyone who is arrested spends time in jail. If a judge determines that he or she is not likely to run away, the arrested person may be allowed to post bail. Posting bail is putting up a sum of money determined by the court to guarantee that the person will appear at the time of trial. The bail may be in the form of a bond purchased from a bail bond agent. If the person shows up, the money is returned. If he or she jumps bail, that is, fails to show up for the trial, the money is given up.

The system of corrections in the United States is complex. Adding to the complexity of the system is the fact that sometimes the federal, state, and local systems mingle. Some federal prisoners serve time in state or county prisons in order to take advantage of special programs that might help their rehabilitation.

Young people also get into trouble with the law. Because federal law prohibits locking a young person up with adult inmates, most juvenile offenders are kept in separate facilities. The exception is young criminals whose cases are so serious that they are being tried as adults.

4

When Juveniles
Go to Prison

Tahir Toombs lived in the New York City borough of Queens. When he was thirteen, he pleaded guilty to murder and was sentenced to nine years to life in prison. Tahir had killed more than once.

His first victim had challenged Tahir for stealing a gold necklace. Tahir shot him in the back with a .380 caliber semiautomatic handgun. Nine days later he killed a cab driver during a robbery for the driver's cab fares.[1]

Tahir will probably spend a long time behind bars. He is part of the growing number of young criminals entering state corrections systems.

Although more boys are arrested for delinquency, girls also commit crimes and get sent to detention facilities. There are many reasons why girls commit crimes. They grow up in the same environment of poverty, family breakdown, and hopelessness as young men. These are all factors that may contribute to criminal behavior. In addition, many girls are abused physically, emotionally, and sexually. Surveys of young female offenders indicate that in 50 to 70 percent of the cases, they have been abused.[2]

Youth crime is nothing new, but nowadays it appears that there are more young criminals who are responsible for serious, violent crimes.

Why has this occurred?

One authority, professor Alfred Blumstein of Carnegie Mellon University, told Congress that a major cause of youth violence is the growing role of drug markets. He said that when crack, a particularly addictive form of cocaine, was introduced around 1985, many inner-city young people were recruited into selling the drug. They carried guns to protect themselves and the drugs they were selling. This brought more guns into the youth community, both for protection and for status. More guns lead to increased crime. Young people who are not trained in gun safety are more likely to shoot without being concerned about the consequences.[3]

Other reasons include the breakdown of the family, lack of parental supervision, lack of jobs, and exposure to too much violence in movies and in television.

Unfortunately, the problem may be getting worse. It is estimated that from 1996 to 2005, the number of teens in the United States will increase by 14 percent. Many of these will be disadvantaged youth who are more at risk for violent behavior.[4]

This increase will add to the population approximately 1 million boys age fourteen to seventeen years. Of these it is estimated that at least 6 percent, or 30,000 youths, may commit violent crimes such as rape, murder, and armed robbery. Lacking adult guidance in their lives, some of the young criminals may be more vicious. New prisons will probably be needed for these offenders.[5]

Before the nineteenth century, young people were imprisoned with adult convicts. Many people were concerned about the bad influence older, hardened criminals might have on young people. They also felt that young people were more likely to be rehabilitated or changed if they were kept in a separate facility. As a result, in the early part of the nineteenth century, authorities began to separate children from the general prison population.

In 1825 the first House of Refuge was established in New York, patterned after a House of Refuge in Germany. Rather than focusing on punishment, the New York House of Refuge was set up to provide the delinquent youth with education. After a young person was released from the House of Refuge, he was assigned an officer who monitored his behavior. If he lapsed back into criminal activities, he would lose his freedom.[6]

The first House of Refuge was a harsh place. Life was organized with strictly enforced times for eating, working, and studying. Conversation was forbidden. After the boys were locked up in their cells at night, there was no noise, because silence was enforced. When a young person did something wrong, he was beaten with a stick or a whip, deprived of a meal, or placed in a solitary cell.[7]

The House of Refuge led the way to building state institutions to deal with young delinquents. Public training schools for the young were established in New York and Massachusetts in 1847.[8]

By 1857 there were more than twenty thousand young offenders in seventeen reformatories, also called

51

reform schools. In 1876, Elmira State Reformatory in New York opened with an educational program that was designed to rehabilitate, or reform, young offenders.

In the end, however, it was impossible to show that the more humane treatment given young men at Elmira Reformatory worked any better than the harsher treatments at conventional prisons. Because they were being forced to learn, many of the young prisoners did not want to take advantage of the educational opportunities.[9]

By the beginning of the twentieth century, life in America was becoming more complex. The way young offenders were treated varied from state to state. Most state reformatories were patterned after the House of Refuge. Several states, including New York, even tried putting young prisoners on ships that completely removed them from society. These were called school ships.

Young African Americans who came into the system had a particularly hard time because few private institutions would accept them. In public institutions, they were segregated from whites.

In some places young delinquents were placed in foster homes or in group homes. In Los Angeles County, El Retiro School provided young people with self-government and modes of positive self-expression such as theater, writing, and a school newspaper. There were also some privately run institutions.[10]

In the mid-1940s, a report to the mayor of New York City pointed out the problems in the Shelter for Dependent, Neglected and Delinquent Children. This shelter was run by an organization called the New York Society for the Prevention of Cruelty to Children.

The city was shocked to learn that the children in the shelter were living in crowded conditions and were sometimes treated cruelly. Those who misbehaved were placed in solitary confinement in cells that had cockroaches and rats. Not all the young people who were living in the shelter were criminals. Some had been taken away from their families because of parental neglect.

To correct the problems of that shelter, the city built Youth House, which opened in the early 1950s. A facility for girls was built in the Bronx. In 1957 a new Youth House for Boys was opened, but soon it, too, was overcrowded. Overcrowded conditions sometimes led to riots. "We have room for 105 girls, but there were 190 in it," commented the assistant director of Youth House for Girls in 1961, after a particularly serious riot took place there.

Although some people complained that the inmates of these facilities were coddled, the opposite was true.[11]

In the early 1960s, author Larry Cole visited Youth House. He discovered that a large majority of the inmates were there for theft or truancy from school. Some were runaways. Some of the inmates had not had a trial, and in some cases they were there because someone—a parent, the schools, or the police—had filed a complaint. At that time, young people did not have the same protection under the Constitution as adults.[12]

Constitutional Rights of Young People

Before the nineteenth century, seven was considered to be the age of reason. Children younger than seven were thought to be incapable of criminal intent. By the time a

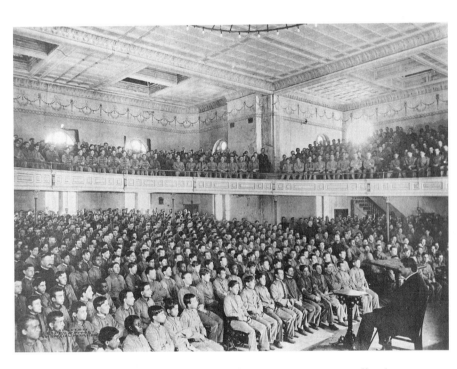

At Elmira Reformatory in New York, young inmates were offered an
opportunity for education.

child reached seven, however, he or she could be tried in a criminal court and could be sentenced to prison or even death if found guilty.

The first juvenile court in the United States was started in Cook County, Illinois, in 1899. It was believed that the state had the power and the responsibility to protect children whose parents were not supervising them adequately. This concept, called the doctrine of *parens patriae*, gave the state the right to get involved in children's lives in a way that was different from the treatment of adult offenders.

By 1925 all but two states had juvenile courts. These courts were based on the belief that young people could be trained to become productive citizens. Rehabilitation has always been a goal of the juvenile justice system. Juvenile courts had jurisdiction over all young people under the age of eighteen who were charged with committing crimes. The young person could be tried as an adult only if the juvenile court waived or surrendered its jurisdiction.

Because the courts were based on the desire to protect juveniles, proceedings were less formal. The due process protections provided by the Constitution were not considered necessary. The judge made the decision on how a case was handled. Representation by an attorney was not thought to be necessary. By the 1960s it had become clear that the system was not fair.

Starting in the early 1960s, the juvenile courts became more formal and began to resemble adult criminal courts.[13] A number of decisions by the Supreme Court made changes in the juvenile justice system.

In 1967, a Supreme Court decision called In re *Gault*

ruled that juveniles have four basic rights in hearings that could lead to their imprisonment. These are the right to notice, the right to legal counsel, the right to question witnesses, and protection against self-incrimination.

The decision involved the case of Gerald Gault, a fifteen-year-old from Arizona who was on probation for committing a minor property offense. While on probation, he and a friend made a crank call to a neighbor in which they made obscene comments. After they were identified and arrested, the court sentenced Gault to stay in a training school until he reached the age of twenty-one. An adult who might have committed a similar crime would have been fined fifty dollars or given two months in jail.

The Supreme Court ruled that Gault's constitutional rights had been violated. He had not received a notice of the charges, nor had he been advised by an attorney. He also had not been able to question witnesses. The Court said that Gault was punished rather than helped by the juvenile court. It said that the manner in which Gault's case had been handled clearly violated the due process clause of the Fourteenth Amendment to the Constitution.

In another landmark decision, *McKeiver* v. *Pennsylvania* (1971), the Court ruled that the Fourteenth Amendment did not require jury trials in juvenile courts. Joseph McKeiver, sixteen, had been charged with robbery and receiving stolen goods after he and other teens had chased three youths and robbed them of twenty-five cents. His attorney's request for a trial by jury had been denied.[14]

Another question that has faced the court is whether

56

detaining a young person before trial violates his or her constitutional rights.

In 1977 Gregory Martin, a fourteen-year-old, was arrested and charged with robbery, assault, and possession of a weapon. He and two others were accused of hitting a boy on the head with a loaded gun and stealing his jacket. He was held before his trial because the court believed there was a serious risk that if released, he might commit another crime. His attorney filed a motion to reverse the order, arguing that holding him before trial was punishing him before he was found guilty. In 1984, in the case *Schall* v. *Martin*, the Supreme Court ruled that holding Martin in jail was constitutional because it protected both the juvenile and society. In this decision the Court again pointed to the importance of the concept of *parens patriae*, which states the interest of the government in promoting the welfare of juveniles.[15]

In summary, the juvenile defendant has the right to counsel by an attorney, to question witnesses, and to protection from self-incrimination. Guilt should be established beyond a reasonable doubt. Trial by jury is not required, because it might violate the privacy that is traditional to juvenile proceedings. Young people can be detained before a trial in juvenile court if it is decided that releasing them might pose a danger either to themselves or to society.

The Juvenile Court System

Before a young offender is sent to a detention facility or a prison, he or she passes through the juvenile court system. Although the Constitution offers guidelines that all states must observe, the individual states determine the age limits of offenders to be tried in juvenile court. For example, in Connecticut, New York, and North Carolina, only defendants under the age of fifteen can be tried in juvenile court. In many other states such as California, Florida, New Jersey, and Pennsylvania, the top age for juvenile court is seventeen. After that age, an offender is considered an adult and is tried in adult criminal court.

If a juvenile has committed a very serious crime such as murder, rape, or arson, the juvenile court may decide to send the case to the adult criminal court.

When a young offender is arrested, a law enforcement officer decides whether the case should be sent to the justice system or whether it should be sent to an alternative program. In 1992, 30 percent of the cases were handled within the police department and the juvenile was then released. Two thirds of the arrested juveniles were sent on to juvenile court. Because federal law discourages local police from holding juveniles in the same facilities as adults, a young person must not be held in areas that are within sight or sound of adult inmates.

The next step is for the young person to go to a hearing before a judge. This hearing usually takes place within twenty-four hours following arrest. If the young offender is to be tried, the judge determines whether the case will go to juvenile court or to the adult criminal system. The judge considers the seriousness of the crime, the young person's prior criminal history, and whether or not the youth's behavior is likely to improve if he or she is treated in the less harsh juvenile system. The final decision is up to the judge.

Even if a young person is sent to juvenile court, depending on the crime, there is a good possibility that the case will be dismissed. Rather than standing trial, the young person may be required to pay the victim for damages, attend school regularly, observe curfew laws, or go into drug counseling if the offense is drug related. If the juvenile fails to live up to what he or she has promised, the case may be reopened.[16]

Sometimes a juvenile is given probation, which may include other requirements such as drug counseling, spending weekends in a detention center, or community service. The probation is monitored carefully. In 1992, six out of ten juvenile defendants were sentenced to probation.

More serious cases are sent to a detention center. Today, some juvenile detention centers look like adult prisons. Some seem like a camp or a group home. Some are run by the state or local government. Others are private. The average length of time a young person might stay in one of these facilities is five months, although some young people are held much longer.

In 1991, thirty-six thousand young people were held in public long-term facilities, and thirty-four thousand were held in privately operated long-term facilities. Three quarters of those in public facilities were in institutions, mostly training schools. Eighty percent of those in private facilities were in more open facilities called halfway houses.[17]

Status and Delinquency Offenders

Status offenses are law violations committed by juveniles that would not be considered crimes if they were committed by an adult. These violations include

59

drinking, truancy, staying out beyond curfew, running away from home, and being out of the control of parents.

Most juveniles held in public detention facilities have been convicted of delinquency offenses, which are crimes against people or property, or drug offenses. In 1991 it was estimated that as many as 95 percent of young offenders had committed crimes of delinquency. A much smaller number, 5 percent, were charged with status offenses.

In the past, status offenders were locked up with juveniles who had committed more serious crimes. In the case of *Harris* v. *Caledine* in 1977, the West Virginia Supreme Court of Appeals ruled that the rights of Gilbert Harris had been violated. Harris had committed the status offense of being absent from school without permission. He had been placed in a secure facility with juveniles who had been involved in more serious crimes. The court said that this violated the due process and equal protection clauses of the state constitution. They also said it was cruel and unusual punishment, which is against the law.[18]

Today, the way status offenders are treated varies from state to state. Most of the time efforts are made to keep the young person out of the criminal justice system. In about one out of five of these cases, however, the young person ends up in juvenile court. More girls are involved in status offenses than in delinquency cases involving criminal charges. While only 15 percent of the delinquency cases processed in 1992 were girls, 42 percent of the status offense cases involved females.[19]

Since 1975 the number of status offenders held in secure prisons has dropped dramatically. Status offenders who do find themselves in secure prisons include those

60

who have broken valid court orders and those who have run away after having been put in a residential setting by court order.[20]

Which Youth End up in Juvenile Prison?

Many of the cases in which young defendants end up in juvenile detention involve drugs. Older youth are more likely to be imprisoned, and boys are more likely to end up in prison than are girls. In 1992, males made up 81 percent of all delinquency cases and 86 percent of those sent to some form of detention.

Race also is a factor. Cases involving African Americans charged with drug offenses were those most likely to be sent to a juvenile detention center.

Youths who have committed serious crimes such as murder make up a minority of the total population of detained juveniles. In California about 16 percent of the juvenile court caseload consists of murderers and other violent youths. Some of these receive lighter sentences because of their age. One teen who killed his employers, a couple who owned a Baskin-Robbins ice cream store, is serving time in the California Youth Authority. He will probably be released when he turns twenty-five. Others are serving similar terms although their crimes were less violent. George, who had been abused and neglected as a child, was found guilty of participating in a home-invasion robbery. Although he did not kill anyone, he, too, may be in prison until he reaches twenty-five.[21]

Detention centers can range from camps located at a distance from the young person's home to facilities that in many ways resemble adult prisons. Young inmates go to

61

school where they are helped to develop academic and vocational skills that will help them to function when they go back into society. There are periods of relaxation when they can play sports.

A detention center is still a prison. Inmates must keep a strict daily schedule. They are not allowed to come and go freely. Gang affiliations may still exist inside, and violence can break out. Forced homosexuality, fights, and beatings may occur.

The experience of being young and in prison is best described by those who have been there.

Malcolm Braly, a former inmate who served many years inside state prisons, experienced his first imprisonment when he was still in high school. He had been sent to a training camp for delinquent boys. He wrote, "If a boy showed any pride or distinction of bearing he was routinely beaten to humble him and train him to at least act as if he were frightened."[22]

A young girl serving time for grand theft auto said, "Well as for my being in jail, well, truthfully, it's not all that bad in here. It's just depressing, especially when it's time to go into our cells during lock up. The only things that I miss are my loved ones, especially my boyfriend. It's not fun being in here and I guarantee you no one in here likes it."[23]

K, a boy serving time for attempted armed robbery said, "I've never been arrested before. . . . Going to school and getting good grades was always too hard for me. But, Buddy, you ain't never seen nothin' harder than doing time in jail."[24]

5

Inside Prison Walls

After an adult has been found guilty of a felony, he or she is often sentenced to spend time in a state or federal prison. If the person has committed a crime in violation of state law, the department of corrections of the state determines the location where the sentence will be served. Men and women are housed in separate prisons. The prisoner will probably be a long way from home because many state prisons are located far from cities. It is often very difficult for families and friends to visit.

The typical prison is a sterile, grim place. High double chain-link fences topped with barbed wire or high walls surround the buildings. Guard towers are placed around the edges of the compound so that guards can watch the prison and its yards at all times.

The prison compound is made up of buildings with thick walls and more than one story. Each floor contains cells, which are small rooms built to house one or two inmates. The cell is sparsely furnished with a bunk, washbasin, and toilet. When the prisoner is asleep at night, he is locked behind bars.

Each floor probably has a television room, a game room, and a group shower. The different units or blocks are separated by grills or sliding barred gates that can be locked. Outdoors there is an exercise yard, which may include a baseball diamond, track, and tennis or handball courts. If there is a grassy area, it is kept closely cut so that inmates cannot hide drugs or weapons.

When a prisoner first arrives, he or she is stripped and given a body-cavity search to see whether the inmate is smuggling contraband such as drugs. In some cases the prisoner is given prison attire. In other prisons an inmate may wear his or her own clothes. The prisoner is assigned to a cell.

A Day in Prison

The new inmate soon finds that life in the prison is regimented and follows a routine. A normal day begins early, around 7:00 A.M., when the cell doors are unlocked. Prisoners are released at fifteen-minute intervals to go to breakfast in the chow hall. They are not all released at once, because that would cause crowding in the chow line, which could lead to a possible disturbance.

All prisoners are expected to keep busy. Some work and others attend classes to finish high school or junior college. After breakfast, the prisoners go to their jobs in one of the prison workshops or attend classes. Lunch is served between 11:30 and 12:30. In the afternoon the prisoners return to their jobs or studies. In the late afternoon a headcount is taken. Dinner follows. After dinner, inmates exercise, socialize, or watch television.

Dean Phillip Carter, a murderer who is serving time on California's death row in San Quentin prison, described an inmate's few personal possessions on his home page, "Dead Man Talkin'" on the World Wide Web: "The prison gives you your meals, clean laundry (once a week), soap, tooth powder, typing paper (about 10 sheets), a pencil stub (exchanged for an old one) or an ink pen filler, and two rolls of toilet paper. These are issued every 1st and 15th of the month."[1]

Work and Study in Prison

Most prisons offer inmates an opportunity to work and study. Prison officials believe that keeping busy helps keep the prison population under control.

Working also helps shorten a convict's stay in prison by reducing the sentence by as much as half. Prisoners also earn a small amount of money for their work. With their wages they may buy small items from the prison store.

In California, prisoners manufacture their clothing and the furniture in their cells. They harvest crops, bake bread, and cook their own food. In addition, they make office furniture used in state government offices, and they restore fire engines, trucks, and other equipment used in local government.

Prisoners also can learn special skills that will help them get a job after release. California prisons operate the only place west of the Mississippi where Braille machines, which help the blind read, can be repaired. Prisoners can also learn a trade such as auto repair, masonry, or meat cutting. Inmates who have not completed high school can work on their diplomas. Some even take community college courses leading to a degree.[2]

One of the country's most progressive programs is the Governor's Community Work Program in North Carolina. In that state, inmates have cleared tire dumps where mosquitoes and snakes had nested. Also, they chopped away underbrush in a state park so that endangered woodpeckers could return to their former nesting places.[3]

Many prisoners try to maintain as normal a life as possible. On weekends, families and friends may come to visit. Some inmates may even get married in prison. In some states, if prisoners have a record of good behavior and are in work or training programs, they may be eligible for family visits. In some California prisons, family visits last forty-eight hours. Inmates and any combination of their children, parents, grandparents, and legal spouses can stay in small cottages or house trailers inside the prison grounds during the two days. It is believed that prisoners have better behavior if they have the possibility of a family visit to look forward to.[4]

Problems in Prison

In spite of the opportunities to work and study, life in prison is still monotonous at best and dangerous at worst. To pass the time, some inmates take up hobbies such as writing or art. Others watch hours of television. Most guards and prison officials say that television is not a luxury. They believe that it calms prisoners who might otherwise become violent.

An inmate from Soledad prison in California gardens under the watchful eye of a guard. The prisoners perform public service by keeping a section of the Monterey Bay coastline clean and well tended.

Prison life also can be dangerous. Fights break out between inmates, sometimes causing serious injuries or even death. Although drugs are forbidden in prison, prisoners seem to find a way to smuggle them in. Homosexuality, often forced, is a fact of life in prison. Gangs cause problems. Occasionally the tension breaks out into rioting.

Drugs in Prison

American prisons are filled with individuals who are serving terms because they were convicted of selling or transporting drugs. Other inmates were under the influence of drugs when they committed their crimes.

Approximately one third of prisoners serving time in state prisons and two fifths of juveniles in long-term state-operated facilities admit that they were under the influence of an illegal drug at the time they committed their crimes.

When a person is arrested, he or she is routinely tested for drug use. In a program that tested males for drug use at the time of arrest, it was discovered that the percentage testing positive ranged from 47 percent in Phoenix to 79 percent in Philadelphia. Females who tested positive ranged from 44 percent in San Antonio to 85 percent in Manhattan, New York.[5]

Even though prisons try very hard to keep drugs out, inmates find ways to get them. Prisoners may have to submit to periodic body-cavity searches. Inmates who return from temporary releases are questioned, searched, and required to change their clothing for prison attire.

Visitors are also patted down and questioned. If they

are suspected of bringing drugs or drug paraphernalia into the prison, they may have to undergo a body-cavity search. Sometimes even the guards or other staff members have been guilty of smuggling drugs into prisons.

The 1990 census revealed that seven out of eight prisons require prisoners to take urine tests. The drugs that were discovered in the tests were marijuana, cocaine, methamphetamines, and heroin.[6]

Homosexuality in Prison

Homosexuality is another common aspect of prison life.

When people are locked up for a long period of time with only a small amount of communication with the outside world, they still crave human contact. Because prisoners are segregated by gender, the relationships that develop are often homosexual in nature. Even inmates who would be heterosexual outside the prison engage in homosexual acts inside prison.

Young inmates may be taken advantage of by older inmates. They may submit to sexual relationships in return for protection. The weak are often forced to submit to sexual advances rather than getting beaten up or raped.

Barry was a young inmate who was arrested in California at the age of sixteen. He was charged and convicted of assault and robbery, and by the age of seventeen, he was sent to prison. When he was admitted to state prison, he was first held in a special dormitory for young inmates who might be at risk in the larger prison population.

It was decided to send Barry to a prison reserved for

Guards routinely search cells for drugs and other forbidden items.

younger, hard-core inmates. The first night in this prison, his nineteen-year-old cellmate beat and raped him. He was later transferred to a medium-security prison. Here, he was approached by an inmate named Ben. Ben offered to protect Barry from other inmates in exchange for a steady sexual relationship. Barry, who had five years to serve on his sentence, felt pressured to accept Ben's offer. Before going to prison, Barry had never had sexual experiences with other males.[7]

Because homosexual activities are forbidden in prison, it is hard to know how often they occur. Between 1979 and 1980, authors Wayne S. Wooden and Jay Parker did a study of sexual behavior in a medium-security prison in California that had a population of 2,500 men. Of these men, 80 percent said they were heterosexual, or had a preference for the opposite sex. Over half of these men, 55 percent, reported that they had homosexual relationships while in prison. Fourteen percent had been forced to have sex against their will.[8]

Homosexual behavior also occurs at women's prisons although most of the time it does not involve rape or other force.

Although guards report homosexual activity and inmates are punished if they are caught, it remains a part of life in prison. It often leads to jealousy and fights between inmates.

Violence in Prison

Violence is a regular occurrence in prison. There are several reasons for this. First, many of the people in prison are serving time for violent crimes. It is not unexpected, then, that their violent behavior would continue during incarceration. Another cause is overcrowding. People do not lose their biases and prejudices when they enter prison. Prejudice is hatred of people from other races or religions. Prejudice and racism frequently cause fights in prisons and jails.

In 1996, overcrowding and prejudice at a Los Angeles County jail led to a series of fights that left 140 inmates injured. The fights, which involved more than sixteen hundred prisoners, were the result of long-standing arguments over power between African-American and Latino inmates. In one fight, the prisoners attacked each other with weapons made from pieces of broken urinals, beds, and light fixtures. The jail, which houses ten thousand inmates, held many violent prisoners. Because other jails were overcrowded, the prisoners were housed in this jail, which had 125-man dormitories instead of cells. Understaffing of prison guards also helped create the explosive environment. Prison officials said that the three-strikes laws, which require mandatory imprisonment after a prisoner has three convictions, also played a part. As a result of the new laws, many inmates are more violent.[9]

Because of an unresolved traffic violation, writer and community activist Javier Rodriguez H. (sic) spent a short period of time in another Los Angeles County jail. In a *Los Angeles Times* editorial, he described the lengthy booking process, the overcrowded holding tanks, the overpowering heat, and the irritation that boiled over into violence. Guards, he wrote, added to the tension.

"The slightest inmate stare, murmur or mistake can bring a threat, a slap or a shove against the wall by the overzealous guards. . . . In some cases—I saw two—the inmate is then isolated, stripped and roughed up some more."[10]

Guards or correctional officers have their own point of view. Working in a prison is a dangerous job.

In a segment on the CBS news program *Forty-Eight Hours*, guards at Lucasville State Prison, a maximum-security institution in Ohio, described their working conditions. One guard described prisoners throwing feces at correctional officers and insulting them with catcalls. Another guard said he had contracted tuberculosis, a serious disease, from prisoners and had then passed the illness to his newborn son.

"They intimidate me as far as fear goes, losing my life or being maimed," a third guard said.

"My greatest fear is dying in there. I don't want to die in there," another said.[11]

Gangs, mostly organized along racial lines, also operate in prison. The prison gangs are involved in all sorts of crimes ranging from extortion to contract murders. Extortion is threatening a person in order to get money or some other favor. Prison gangs are also involved in drug trafficking. Some prisoners are loyal to the gang they were in outside of prison. Others join prison gangs such as the Mexican Mafia, the Black Muslims, or the Aryan Brotherhood.[12]

Inside the prison, inmates often do not hide their gang affiliation. At Rikers Island in New York City, gang members show their affiliation by wearing beads around their necks. Latin Kings wear black and gold. The Netas wear white, red, and black beads. The Latin Kings are neighborhood and prison gangs in Chicago and

Connecticut; in New York they are mainly a prison gang. The Netas started as a prison gang in Puerto Rico in the 1970s.[13]

When violence boils over, riots break out. To restore order, the prison may be put into lockdown. The prisoners are deprived of their privileges, which may include recreation, classes, and visits from family.

At the federal maximum-security penitentiary in Marion, Illinois, lockdown is a way of life. Between 1980 and 1983 there were fourteen attempted escapes, ten group disruptions, thirty-three attacks against correctional officers, and fifty-eight attacks against other inmates. Nine inmates and two guards were killed. Since that time, the nation's most dangerous prisoners, gang leaders and troublemakers, have been kept in individual cells. They have no group recreation, classes, or rehabilitation programs. For most of the day, prisoners are kept locked up in their cells.

Critics of Marion say that the lockdown is cruel punishment. They point to the historical evidence that keeping prisoners in isolation does not work. Those in favor of the lockdown say that it has cut down on violence and is an effective way to control the most violent inmates.[14]

Health Problems in Prison

Many inmates enter prison in poor health. Those who have lived in poverty have not had access to good health care. Because prisoners live in close conditions, disease can spread rapidly.

Tuberculosis; HIV, the human immunodeficiency

virus; and AIDS are serious problems in prison. Tuberculosis is a highly infectious disease that is transmitted through the air. In a 1992–93 survey made for the Centers for Disease Control and the National Institute of Justice, it was discovered that inmates had a tuberculosis rate that was thirteen times the rate of the general population in the United States. More women were infected than men. Inmates are not the only ones at risk. Because the disease is contagious, the survey found that forty-three prison workers had tuberculosis and about six hundred more were infected with TB.[15]

The human immunodeficiency virus, HIV, can be transmitted by unprotected sexual contact or through sharing a needle to inject drugs.

The occurrence of AIDS in prisons has been increasing faster than in the general population. In 1992 there were 18 cases of AIDS per 100,000 people in the United States. In prisons, the rate was 362 cases per 100,000 inmates. This rate was 100 percent higher than the rate reported in 1990 when 181 inmates per 100,000 tested positive for the illness. It is also occurring at a greater rate within the prison population. By early 1993, the number of inmates who were dying of AIDS or AIDS-related diseases was 3,474.[16]

Being infected with a highly contagious disease such as AIDS or tuberculosis affects prisoners' lives in many ways. Those who are infected are isolated from healthy inmates. This means that they may not be able to participate in opportunities for recreation, education, rehabilitation, and work that other inmates have.

Prisoners' attitudes toward their illnesses also can cause problems for prison officials. Some inmates view

In this Connecticut prison, men are fed cafeteria-style.

medical care as something that is done to them without their permission. Others may fear that authorities are not providing the right care at the right time. Those infected may resent their loss of privileges and restriction of movement. Sometimes these resentments lead to violence. In one prison, inmates rioted because they did not want to be tested for TB.[17]

Parole

A high percentage of inmates are released on parole before serving out all the years of their sentences. Parole is a release from prison with conditions. Parole is similar to probation, which is a sentence served in a community setting rather than prison.

Parole boards meet regularly at state and federal prisons to look at inmates' records to see who might be eligible for parole. They talk to prison officials, and they interview the inmate to check his or her emotional state and attitude. They look at whether the inmate has gotten into trouble while in prison.

If parole is granted, the parolee signs a contract stating the conditions of his or her release. The conditions might include promising not to leave his or her county of residence, not to use drugs or alcohol, not to drive a car, and not to possess a gun.

He or she must promise to report to a parole officer, who will enforce the rules of the probation. The officer can search the parolee's house without a warrant. Parole may be suspended if the officer believes that the parolee is breaking the law. If this occurs, the criminal may be sent back to prison.[18]

The first year following a parolee's release is the most important, studies show. Most violations of parole occur shortly after release. Those with a history of arrests prior to coming to prison were the individuals most likely to break parole. Poverty also plays a part. The more affluent a parolee is, the less likely he or she is to violate parole. The emotional support of one's family also helps keep a parolee from getting into more trouble. Getting a regular job is helpful, too. Authorities try to put parolees into daytime jobs that have regular hours.[19]

Because many employers have prejudices against hiring an employee who has served time in prison, good jobs are often hard to find.

People also may not want certain inmates, especially rapists and child molesters, to move to their communities.

Some inmates will never be paroled. Lifers, those who have been given a life sentence without possibility of parole, and those who have received a penalty of death must face spending the rest of their lives in a prison setting.

6

Life in Prison/
Death Row

Two groups of inmates will never reenter society. One group is made up of inmates serving life sentences without possibility of parole. The other group is made up of inmates on death row.

Life in Prison Without Possibility of Parole

Eric and Lyle Menendez were rich young men from Beverly Hills, California, who brutally murdered both their mother and father. They claimed their parents had abused them, both emotionally and sexually. In the brothers' first trial for murder, the jury could not come to a decision of guilt or innocence. In the second trial, in 1996, however, the jury found them guilty of first-degree murder and sentenced them to spend life in prison without possibility of parole. First-degree murder is killing with premeditation or planning.

79

In American prisons the number of inmates serving life sentences without possibility of parole has been increasing. As of 1992 there were 65,281 men and 2,482 women serving life sentences in state and federal prisons. Forty-four thousand were convicted of first- or second-degree murder. Twenty-two thousand five hundred were in prison for other offenses, including kidnapping, drug offenses, sexual assault, or robbery, or were habitual offenders. Out of the total, 10,843 men and 358 women were serving sentences of life without possibility of parole.[1]

During the 1980s, concerns about rising crime led to demands that criminals serve longer terms. By 1995, sentences in the twenty- to twenty-five-year range had become routine. Life sentences without possibility of parole also became more common. Of the eighty thousand inmates serving life sentences in 1994, more than ten thousand were serving natural-life sentences. Natural-life sentences require the inmate to spend the rest of his or her life in prison.

Because more states can send people away for life without parole and because the prison population has been increasing, the total number of lifers will probably continue to increase. Three-strikes laws, which have become popular in recent years, will also add to the number. Under these laws, a criminal who has been convicted of three felony offenses may become ineligible for parole.

Clemency

After serving a part of their sentences, a small number of prisoners who are serving life terms with the possibility of parole may have their sentences shortened. This is accomplished through clemency and commutation.

80

From the guard tower at San Quentin prison in California, officers can watch the shore and land near the prison to keep prisoners from escaping.

Clemency means forgiveness. Long ago, a ruler could pardon or excuse a convict of his or her crime or shorten the time an inmate would have to stay in prison. Clemency does not always mean a full pardon, which would involve giving back to the prisoner rights and property that have been taken away.

In nineteenth-century and early twentieth-century America, clemency was more common than it is today. At that time, it was much harder to shorten one's term through good behavior and parole. Most prisoners, even those serving life sentences, could expect to be granted clemency after being in prison for several years.

In 1975, Catherine "Kitty" Dodds was sentenced to death in the murder-for-hire killing of her husband, an ex-New Orleans policeman. In 1977, the governor of Louisiana granted clemency, commuting or reducing her sentence from death to life in prison. She escaped from prison in 1980 but was soon recaptured. Claiming that she had been a battered wife, she again asked for clemency. Her life sentence was reduced by the governor to thirty years in 1986. Seventeen years after her husband had been killed, she was finally released from prison.[2]

State governors and the president of the United States have the right to grant clemency. Usually, a prisoner must have approval of both the pardon board and the governor to receive clemency. The pardon board is a committee of citizens appointed by the governor that reviews a prisoner's record to decide whether or not to recommend that the governor grant clemency. Usually, the recommendation is passed if a simple majority of the clemency board agrees. In the case of a prisoner serving a life sentence, the clemency is called a commutation.

Because a commutation involves shortening a sentence, inmates call it a "time cut."[3]

In deciding whether or not to commute an inmate's life sentence, the pardon board considers how the person has behaved while in prison. Has she followed the rules? Has he taken courses or training that would indicate the possibility of rehabilitation?

Once the recommendation for a commutation is decided by the pardon board, the paperwork goes to the governor's office, where it is reviewed before being given to the governor for his or her signature. It may reach the governor's desk in a few days, or it may lie around for several years. The recommendation takes effect after the governor signs the commutation.

If an inmate has already served a number of years of the sentence and has a record of credits for good behavior, it is possible that a commutation means an immediate release from prison. This is called a "cut to time served."

Most lifers, however, are not immediately released after receiving a commutation. Their sentence might be cut from life to sixty to ninety years with parole eligibility after serving one third of the sentence. They would be released after serving twenty to thirty years of their sentence.[4]

Some people argue that releasing older inmates makes sense. They believe that older inmates are less threatening to society. Keeping them in prison takes up room that could be better used to house younger criminals who are a danger to others. Aging prisoners also cost the state more money because they have more serious health problems. They are also more likely to be victimized and injured by younger inmates. Because of longer sentences, prison populations are becoming older in many states. As of March 1994, Angola State Prison in Louisiana held 2,429 prisoners who were older than thirty-five.[5]

Death Row

Currently, thirty-eight states allow capital punishment.[6] In these states, prisoners sentenced to death are kept in a special part of the prison called death row.

Before a person is actually executed, there is a long process of state and federal appeals. If an inmate decides to fight a death sentence, the appeals process can take many years.

One of the reasons for the delays is the shortage of attorneys who are trained to represent inmates on death row. In California, attorneys who are qualified to represent inmates in such cases must have gained four years of criminal defense experience. They also have to attend special classes on appellate work and must have completed seven appeals cases. The shortage of appeals lawyers exists nationwide. In Pennsylvania approximately half of the 196 condemned inmates had no lawyers.

Some of the reasons attorneys do not want to work with death row appeals are low pay, long hours, and lack of prestige. It is also frustrating to spend a long period of time preparing an appeal for a criminal who has been convicted of horrible crimes. In most cases the appeal will most likely be denied by the strict higher courts.

In California, the appeal transcripts must be certified for accuracy by the original murder trial judge. Transcripts can be as long as ten thousand pages, each of

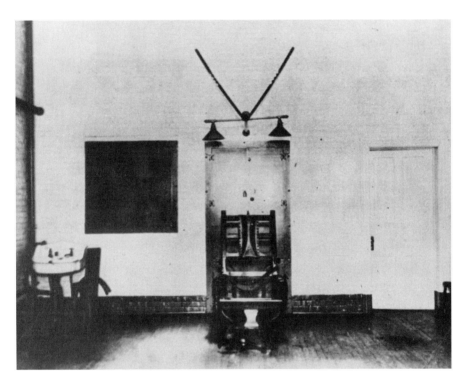

In the past, the electric chair was often used in executions. Today, death by lethal injection is a more common method.

which must be reviewed for errors by all those concerned—the court reporters, court clerk, trial attorneys, and the judge. This alone can add years of delay. Since the death penalty was reinstated in California in 1978, only three people had actually been executed as of April 1996.

Take the example of Dean Phillip Carter, a serial killer who was sentenced to death in 1989 for the murders he committed in 1984. He received a second death penalty in 1991 for raping and killing a woman near San Diego. It took Carter three and a half years to get an appeals lawyer. Seven years after his first death sentence, he had still not filed his appeal because the trial record was being certified.[7]

On the day of the execution, the convict is allowed to visit with his or her family. Then a final meal of the inmate's choosing is served. In many states the execution is done at midnight.

In the United States, the death penalty has been carried out in many different ways. Prisoners have been killed by electric chair, gas chamber, firing squad, and by hanging, and more recently, by lethal injection.

In many states death by lethal injection has replaced the gas chamber or the electric chair. In this form of execution, the prisoner is strapped on a table and is injected with massive overdoses of drugs. As of 1996 thirty-two states used this method of execution. Of the fifty-six people who were executed in the United States in 1995, all but seven died this way.

In spite of the delays, the number of executions in the United States has been steadily increasing. In 1977, after the Supreme Court reinstated the death penalty, only one person was executed. In 1995, fifty-six men were executed in sixteen states. This was the largest annual

number since 1957. Thirty-three were white, twenty-two
were African-American, and one was Asian. Forty-nine of
the executions were carried out by lethal injection: seven
were by electrocution. At the end of 1995, 3054 prisoners were in thirty-four state and federal prisons under the
sentence of death. This was an increase of 5.1 percent
over the previous year.[8]

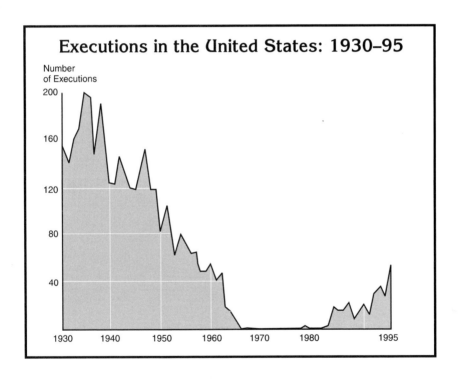

Executions in the United States: 1930–95

The number of executions in the United States has been steadily
increasing since the Supreme Court reinstated the death penalty
in 1977.

87

7

Do Prisons and Harsh Sentences Stop Crime?

Since 1980 the number of prisons and the number of Americans behind bars have been steadily climbing. As of 1994, 5.1 million Americans were serving time in prison, or were on probation. This amounted to 2.7 percent of the population of the United States. Statistics show that since 1980, state and federal prison populations have risen 213 percent.

In spite of building more prisons, most are overcrowded. As of 1995, prisons were filled at 20 percent over capacity. In addition, many of the inmates of jails should be spending time in prison, but there just is not room for them. Prisons are very costly. In 1994, the average cost to keep a person in jail or prison for a year was $25,000.[1]

Because prisons are expensive both in human terms and in money terms, it is necessary to ask some serious questions about their effectiveness.

Do prisons actually help to stop the occurrence of violent crime? Are prisons too luxurious? Are prison terms too lenient? Can prisoners really be rehabilitated so that they will not be a threat to society?

To understand these questions we have to go back to the reasons for incarceration or imprisonment. Is the purpose of prison to punish wrongdoers, or should it rehabilitate those who have broken society's laws, so that they can become law-abiding citizens? In practice, prisons try to serve both purposes.

How Effective Is Rehabilitation?

Because a majority of prisoners do reenter society, it is necessary to give them some training and education so they will not return to a life of crime. At the same time, some individuals have committed crimes so serious that they cannot be trusted to go back into society. Others have shown that they cannot live within the law. Once out of prison, they commit crimes that lead to their return. The tendency to repeat one's offenses is called recidivism. Statistics from the Justice Department show that approximately "62 percent of state prisoners are rearrested within three years of being released from prison."[2]

Rehabilitation means changing a person's habits and attitudes so that he or she will be able to cope in the world. Since the end of the nineteenth century, prisons have tried to reform inmates through training, group therapy, and education.

In recent years, however, public attitude has demanded that prisons punish criminals more strictly, taking away privileges such as attending classes. Many people have complained that prison educational programs cost too much money. In 1994 Congress cut off federal grant money that allowed 27,000 inmates to attend school. The prisoners had used government money called Pell grants to finance their educations.

"The bottom line is that the honest and hard-working are being elbowed out of the way by criminals," said Kay Bailey Hutchison of Texas, the representative who sponsored the new law cutting off funds.[3]

There is another side to the story.

Studies have shown that education, especially at a college level, keeps prisoners from returning to crime. In New York, 45 percent of inmates who did not have college degrees were found likely to return to prison. Of those that had college diplomas, only 26 percent returned. In Texas the statistics were even more striking. Only 13.7 percent of the inmates who earned a junior college degree and 5.6 percent of those who earned a bachelor's degree returned to prison.[4]

"When you eliminate these programs, you are increasing the odds that criminals will re-offend," said Barry Krisberg, president of the National Council on Crime and Delinquency.[5]

Advocates of tough sentences believe that the main function of prisons is to punish. They applaud a jail compound located near Phoenix, Arizona, where 1,000 inmates are housed in tents. In the summer the temperatures rise to 120 degrees. Inmates cannot have long hair or beards. To get out of solitary confinement, some inmates volunteer for work in chain gangs. The chain gangs pick up trash along the highways and

For more than one hundred years, prisons in the United States have tried to reform inmates through training, group therapy, and education.

sometimes dig graves for the poor who are buried in county cemeteries.

"Why should you have a beautiful place to live when you've violated the law? You should be punished, not rewarded," said Sheriff Joe Arpaio, who administers the prison.

Does this harsh treatment work? Even among inmates opinion is divided.

One inmate serving on a chain gang said, "I don't think I want to come back." Another inmate disagreed. "You forget what it's like inside. The day you get out, you forget."[6]

Because tent prisons are inexpensive to build, they are seen as one way to help the problem of overcrowding.

Will Building More Prisons Help Cut Down on Crime?

Many people believe that building more prisons will take criminals off the streets. They argue that crime rates drop when the possibility of being sent to prison is high. Some statistics seem to back up this theory.[7]

In 1980, Michigan voters rejected a proposal to raise income taxes to build new prisons. To reduce prison over-crowding, the governor used his emergency powers to free 10,000 prisoners. A study of 5,762 of the paroled inmates found that one third were rearrested within three years. Twelve had committed murder.[8]

Voter concerns about crime led the Michigan legislature to build twenty-eight new prisons by 1992, at a cost of $900 million. The inmate population increased from

14,392 to 33,062. Serious crime rates declined 9 percent. Robbery and burglary rates dropped 25 percent.[9]

Critics say that building more prisons costs too much. They point out that the corrections' budget in California is growing twice as fast as the state budget. In Michigan as of 1990, 7 percent of the total state revenues were spent on corrections. Critics argue that the crime rate hasn't really changed. They say that there is very little relationship between crime and the rate of imprisonment.[10]

Why is this true?

Some criminologists believe that habitual criminals do not believe they will get caught. This is because only one out of every three crimes is reported to the police. Of these reported crimes, only 20 percent, or approximately seven out of every one hundred crimes, results in an actual arrest.[11]

Prisons Are Expensive

Building more prisons is very costly. The average cost to build a space to house one prisoner is around $48,000 and has been as much as $150,000.[12] Some critics argue that some of these funds should go to fight the causes of crime such as poor education and poverty.

Politicians sometimes support building more prisons because taking a tough position on crime is popular with voters.

"America has embraced vengeance as its criminal-justice philosophy. People don't want solutions to crime, they only want to feel good. That is what politicians are doing, they're making people feel secure," said Wilbert

Rideau, who is serving a life sentence for murder at the Louisiana State Penitentiary at Angola. During his time in prison, Rideau has become famous as a journalist, author, and advocate of prison reform.[13]

In general, people seem to want more prisons, and they do not want them to be pleasant places. They do not appear to be overly concerned about problems such as overcrowding. When they read about prisoners receiving what appear to be luxuries, they become furious.

At Mercer Regional Correctional Facility in western Pennsylvania, 850 prisoners enjoy a full-sized basketball court, a handball area, and volleyball. In the gym there are barbells, weight-lifting machines, stair-type aerobics machines, and nine electronic exercise bicycles.[14]

Prison administrators believe that recreation and education help to change criminal behavior for the better.

In Arizona, state prisons have a tough program where inmates have to obey a strict dress and grooming code. To cut overcrowding, prisoners have to share cells, and inmate labor helps build new prisons, cutting costs. The tough program has cut down on escapes. It has also reduced the costs for Arizona. The state spends 38 percent less than the national average to build a new medium-security cell, and 45 percent less to build a new maximum-security cell.

Opponents say that the statistics do not prove that these methods work. They argue that between 60 and 70 percent of inmates go back to crime once they are out of prison. For over ten years, a model federal prison at Butner, North Carolina, offered prisoners many different forms of rehabilitation. Still, there was no reduction in crime once these inmates returned to society. Also, their job prospects were not improved.[15]

Tough prisons may make some criminals think twice before committing another crime. Other criminals may come out more hardened and vicious than when they entered prison.

Do Prisons Create Criminals?

Prisons have been accused of being schools for crime. Inmates are in contact with other criminals who may teach them more about crime. After a short time in prison, an inmate may learn to accept the prison life. He or she may also feel a sense of bitterness that is later directed back at society.[16]

Inside prison, inmates develop a prisoners' community that has its own set of values. Sociologists have found that a prisoner's indentification with prison values versus "outside" values follows a *U*-shaped path. The longer a person stays in prison, the more he or she identifies with the values of the prison rather than those of the society outside. As a prisoner nears release time, he or she tends to readopt outside values.[17] Prisoners who serve shorter terms are more likely to successfully cope with society's values when they get out.

There is also evidence that children of parents in prison have a greater possibility of ending up in prison themselves at some period in their lives. Several generations of a family may be locked up at any given time. Many boys and girls in the juvenile justice system have parents who are or who have been behind bars. A warden at the California Rehabilitation Center in Norco,

Regimentation has always been a part of prison life. In the dining
hall at this prison, inmates had little choice as to what they were
given to eat.

California, where inmates are treated for substance abuse, estimated that 63 percent of the children whose mothers are in custody end up in jail, too. He also added that it is not as unusual as in the past to see three generations—grandmother, mother, daughter—all locked up at the same time.[18]

Do Longer Sentences Deter Criminals?

Another response to the crime problem is the demand for longer sentences for criminals, especially those who have been convicted before. This has led to the three-strikes laws, in which an offender is given a long sentence after having been convicted of the third felony or serious offense.[19]

In 1994, California voters passed the three-strikes law, which required judges to give a sentence of at least twenty-five years to life to criminals found guilty of a third felony, even if it was a nonviolent offense such as drug dealing. However, this was true only for convicted criminals whose previous convictions were for serious crimes. In 1996, the California Supreme Court gave judges the right to overlook earlier convictions in order to reduce a criminal's sentence.

It was expected that as many as twenty thousand prisoners who had been sentenced to long terms because of the three-strikes law could file appeals.[20]

Critics of the three-strikes law complained that it required building more prisons to hold all the convicts sentenced to life in prison. They argued that the law was too costly.

Those supporting the law argued that criminals who

continue to commit crimes do not deserve to be free. They credited the law with lowering the crime rate.[21]

A study by the Rand Corporation, a California research organization, estimated that three-strikes laws might reduce serious crime by 21 percent but would cost $5.5 billion a year to administer.[22]

Since 1987 many states have laws requiring mandatory minimum sentences. Mandatory minimum sentences are guidelines that went into effect in 1987, after Congress had passed the Sentencing Reform Act of 1984. Before, judges could look at many factors, such as prior arrest records, when sentencing a criminal to prison. With mandatory minimum sentences, the judge is not allowed to consider these factors.[23]

A result of mandatory minimum sentences is that lawbreakers spend more time in prison. In Indiana, for example, burglars and rapists spend 100 percent more time in prison than in the past. Armed robbers serve terms that are 30 percent longer.[24]

Critics say that many mandatory sentences are for nonviolent drug offenses. Sometimes violent offenders such as rapists, robbers, and murderers are released early to make room for nonviolent drug offenders who have been given long mandatory sentences.[25]

Another complaint is that the three-strikes law and mandatory minimum sentencing laws clog the courts.

In Los Angeles County jails, which are severely over-crowded, many convicted offenders are released early because of lack of space. Among those released are drug addicts, car burglars, petty thieves, prostitutes, and those arrested for minor assaults such as bar fights. Of approximately five hundred categories of misdemeanors, only ten—including stalking and some types of sexual assault—keep a person in custody.

Before the three-strikes law took effect in 1994, most felons spent sixty days in jail from the time of arrest to the time of sentencing or acquittal. Many resolved their cases through plea bargains.

Since the three-strikes law, however, this has changed.

"All of a sudden . . . nobody plea bargains," said Paul E. Myron, one of two administrators of Los Angeles County's seven jails, which have a population of 18,000 inmates. "All want to go to jury trial because they can't afford to plead guilty if there is the slightest chance they will be acquitted."[26]

8

Possible Solutions to the Problems of Prison

Most people agree that violent criminals should be locked up in prison. They disagree, however, on how to deal with those who are not violent and those who do not have a long criminal record. Home imprisonment, electronic monitoring, boot camps, embarrassment, closely supervised probation, repaying victims, and community service are other ways lawbreakers may be punished. These alternatives are also a way to deal with those offenders who might become even more hardened if sent to prison. To solve the problems of overcrowding and spiraling costs, some states and communities are turning to private corporations to build and operate their jails and prisons.

Home Imprisonment and Electronic Monitoring

Since 1985 some lawbreakers have served their sentences without actually stepping foot into a prison. As a part of probation, the offender is sentenced to wear an electronic monitor around his or her ankle. The monitor sends signals to a computer in the monitoring company's office. If the person leaves home, the signal is broken. Not following the rules of probation could send the offender to jail.

Computerized telephones are also used to monitor a prisoner's whereabouts. In one system a computer records the prisoner's voice. The computer then calls at random hours and asks questions of the person who answers the phone. If the wrong voice answers the question, the prisoner's probation officer is notified.

A video telephone, or videophone, is another device that monitors offenders. It shows the person in his or her living room. When the special telephone rings, the person has to punch a button that sends an image back to the firm that owns and operates the system. Most offenders prefer this system to spending time in prison.[1]

Another way that prison time is cut is by requiring a convict to live in a halfway house.

A halfway house is a home where a group of offenders live together in a controlled setting. The home is usually located in a residential neighborhood. Some residents have served part of their sentences in a prison before being released to a halfway house. Others are sentenced directly to live in the halfway house rather than in prison.

Even though most halfway houses and residential centers are not locked, those who live there are tightly supervised. The residents can leave to go to school or to work, but they have to check in and check out. At night or when staff shifts change, there is a headcount to make sure that all residents are accounted for. Drugs and

Some lawbreakers are ordered to wear an electronic monitor so that they can serve house arrest rather than going to prison.

alcohol are forbidden, as are all tools that might be used as weapons.[2]

Some halfway houses focus on offenders who have special problems such as drug or alcohol abuse. At the halfway house, these offenders are helped to deal with their addictions. In other facilities, women with preschool children can have their children with them. Day care is provided so that the women can go to work or school during the day.

Some inmates who have had good behavior while in prison may be released before their parole to work or go to school in or near their home communities. They have to stay in a work-release center. These centers have a more natural environment than prison, but the rules inmates must follow help them readjust to society.

Boot Camps

Boot camps are places where offenders, mostly males, are sent to spend a short time in a program that involves strict rules, physical training, and hard labor. The boot camp is designed to scare young offenders away from a life of crime. Most of those who attend have records of earlier arrests.

Boot camp, sometimes called "shock incarceration," is based on military training camps.

At some boot camps, the offender's head is shaved, and his personal possessions are locked up. He is required to wear a uniform. Privileges such as smoking cigarettes are forbidden.

Offenders rise as early as 5:00 A.M. to begin a strenuous physical training program. Inmates clean their barracks as often as twice a day. They cannot speak without permission. Above all, they are not allowed to complain about their chores or the rules.

In Georgia the boot-camp program has been very successful at turning young offenders around. In the first three years of the program, only 20 percent returned to a life of crime.[3]

In southern California, girl offenders may be sent to Camp Scott, one of a handful of military-style boot camps for girls in the country.[4]

Embarrassment or Let the Punishment Fit the Crime

Some judges sentence nonviolent criminals to do something that will shock them or make them embarrassed for what they have done. In some cases, drunk drivers and teenage drug dealers have been sentenced to watch autopsies. Small-time drug dealers may have to work with AIDS patients. A slumlord is ordered to live for a time in one of his own buildings. A criminal may be given the choice of jail time or publishing an ad in the newspaper with an apology for what he or she has done.

Creative sentencing saves taxpayers the money that it would cost to put these people in jail.[5]

A criticism of this kind of sentence is that it is usually reserved for wealthy offenders. Poor people and people with unpopular political or religious beliefs are less likely to receive a creative sentence. Another criticism is that this type of sentence gives judges too much power. It is argued that the judge should follow the laws set down by

105

state and federal legislatures as to criminal sentences for specific crimes. The public likes to think that the law is fair and that similar cases should receive similar punishments.[6]

Those who support creative sentencing believe that it saves money. They point to the high costs of keeping an inmate in prison and the high cost of building a prison cell, which may cost more than building a house. If a person is not a danger to society, they argue, it is better to have him or her working and paying taxes rather than in jail.[7]

They argue that locking criminals up in prisons does not really reduce crime, because only a few of those who commit felony crimes actually end up in prison. Most are still on the street. Also, many crimes are committed by groups such as car theft rings and drug rings. When some of the criminals involved in these operations are sent to prison, others are recruited to take their place. The cycle of crime continues.[8]

These observers believe that it is more effective to design sentences to meet the needs of the victim, the offender, and the community. Such a sentence might involve repayment to the victim; community service; required drug, alcohol, or mental health counseling; or staying in school.[9]

Privatized Prisons

Some prison authorities believe that private firms can do a better job of running prisons than do state and federal governments. In the 1980s, several firms began building and running prisons. This trend is called privatization.

This correctional officer is on duty in the tower at R. J. Donovan
Correctional Facility in San Diego, California.

In the nineteenth and early twentieth centuries, several states had private prisons. Texas leased prisons to private contractors who in turn leased the inmates out to work on farms and in industry. Most were treated harshly, and many died within seven years of their imprisonment. A number of convicts tried to escape, and some committed suicide.[10]

Today, supporters of private prisons believe that they can be built more quickly and for less money than state prisons.

In California, the Department of Corrections needs an average of forty-two months to build a prison. The average cost of a new prison is about $300 million for construction and another $300 million for interest on the money the state has to borrow to build the prison. A private firm in Florida built two 750-bed prisons in less than two years. The private firm also plans to build six prisons in Florida with a total of 4,000 beds for about $140 million.[11]

In 1995, 17 companies in the United States operated 104 prisons. Seal Beach, a small community in Orange County, California, formed a partnership with Correctional Systems Inc., a Texas-based corporation that builds and operates private prisons. The thirty-man jail holds state work-furlough inmates and inmates arrested for drunkenness in nearby communities. Others also held there are federal prison transfers serving out the last months of their sentences. The city saves money because it avoids paying a $176 per inmate fee that Orange County charges for inmates in the main county lockup.[12]

Opponents of private prisons say that government has to look beyond economics in the prison issue.

"Prison is the strongest punishment the state can mete out, short of the death penalty, and it shouldn't be handed over to the profit motive," said Jenni Gainsborough, of the National Prison Project of the American Civil Liberties Union.[13]

Prison-guard unions also oppose the private prisons. They fear that private prisons are more likely to have inmate revolts. The prison professionals believe that a better answer is to upgrade prison management so that those in charge can offer more humane treatment to prisoners.

"We haven't lost a prison (to inmate revolt), but if you bring this (privatization) online, you will lose a prison," said Don Novey, president of the 23,000-member California Correctional Peace Officers Association.[14]

Many people want prisons to solve the problems of crime and criminals. They want to see criminals pay for their crime in conditions that often are harsh. To accomplish this they are willing to use large sums to build more prisons, even though it is evident that many who go to prison return to a life of crime after being released. These same people may not want to spend tax dollars to solve the social problems that contribute to crime.

Others are perhaps overly sympathetic toward criminals. They believe that the court should consider the reasons why a person has become a criminal. These might be racism, poor education, and child abuse. They want to emphasize rehabilitation over punishment.

Because it is difficult to balance the rights of victims and the rights of the prisoners as human beings, prisons are a hard problem for society. Unfortunately, they are a problem that society must face.

The solutions to building and running more efficient prisons are not easy to come by. Should prisons punish or should they rehabilitate? Does fear of going to prison stop people from committing crimes? Do prisons protect society from crime? Should public money be spent to build more prisons, or should funds go toward remedying social problems such as racism, poor education and housing, and abusive and neglectful families, which are seen as causes of crime? What do you think about the serious issues raised by prisons?

Chapter Notes

Chapter 1

1. Isabel Wilkerson, "2 Boys, a Debt, a Gun, a Victim: The Face of Violence," *The New York Times*, May 16, 1994, pp. A1, A14.

2. Tony Perry, "Killer, Now 15, Sentenced to Prison," *Los Angeles Times*, June 19, 1996, p. A3.

3. "Uniform Crime Reports," *Crime in the United States: 1991* (Washington, D.C.: The F.B.I., 1992), p. 217.

4. "Prisons and Jail Inmates, 1995," Office of Justice Programs (Washington, D.C.: U.S. Department of Justice, August 1996), p. 1.

5. Robert James Bidinotto, "Must Our Prisons Be Resorts?" *Reader's Digest*, November 1994, pp. 65–69.

6. Robert James Bidinotto, "Revolving Door Justice: Plague on America," *Reader's Digest*, February 1994, pp. 34–35.

7. Bruce Shapiro, "How the War on Crime Imprisons America," *The Nation*, April 22, 1996, p. 19.

8. "The Cycle of Violence Revisited" (Washington, D.C.: U.S. Department of Justice, February 1996), p. 1.

Chapter 2

1. Vernon Fox, *Introduction to Corrections*, 3rd ed. (Englewood Cliffs, N.J.: Prentice-Hall, Inc., 1985), pp. 3–4.

2. Ibid., p. 7.

3. Lois Warburton, *Prisons* (San Diego: Lucent Books, Inc., 1993) p. 12.

4. Robert J. Wright, "Prison: Historical Background," *Encyclopedia Americana*, international ed. (Danbury, Conn.: Grolier, Inc., 1995), vol. 22, p. 621.

5. J. J. Tobias, *Crime and Police in England, 1700–1900* (New York: St. Martins Press, 1979), pp. 152–155.

6. Wright, p. 622.

7. Warburton, pp. 16–17.

8. Wright, p. 622.

9. Tobias, pp. 150–151.

10. Ibid., pp. 140–145.

11. Warburton, p. 18.

12. Tobias, pp. 160–161.

13. Ibid., pp. 162–163.

14. Ibid., p. 158.

15. Warburton, pp. 19–20.

16. Fox, p. 16.

17. Warburton, p. 22.

18. Edward L. Ayers, *Vengeance & Justice: Crime and Punishment in the 19th-Century American South* (New York: Oxford Press, 1984), pp. 42–48, 52, 58.

19. Ibid., pp. 59–63.

20. Ibid., pp. 65, 66, 67.

21. Warburton, p. 25.

22. Wright, p. 623.

23. Fox, pp. 16–71.

24. Anne E. Weiss, *Prisons: A System in Trouble* (Hillside, N.J.: Enslow Publishers, Inc., 1988), pp. 29–30.

25. Phyllis Elperin Clark and Robert Lehrman, *Doing Time: A Look at Crime and Prisons* (New York: Hastings House Publishers, 1980), pp. 56–57.

26. Warburton, pp. 32–36.

27. Robert James Bidinotto, "Must Our Prisons Be Resorts?" *Reader's Digest,* November 1, 1994, p. 69.

Chapter 3

1. Anne E. Weiss, *Prisons: A System in Trouble* (Hillside, N.J.: Enslow Publishers, Inc., 1988), pp. 35–39.

2. Robert Worth, "A Model Prison," *Atlantic Monthly,* November 1995, pp. 38, 40.

3. Steven J. Martin and Sheldon Ekland-Olson, *Texas Prisons: The Walls Came Tumbling Down* (Austin: Texas Monthly Press, 1987), pp. 5–6.

4. Phyllis Elperin Clark and Robert Lehrman, *Doing Time: A Look at Crime and Prisons* (New York: Hastings House Publishers, 1980), p. 59.

5. Martin and Ekland-Olson, pp. 6–7.

6. Lois Warburton, *Prisons* (San Diego: Lucent Books, Inc., 1993), pp. 30–31.

7. *Corrections, Public Safety, Public Service* (Sacramento: California State Department of Corrections, 1993), pp. 6–8.

8. "Prisoners in 1994," *Bureau of Justice Statistics Bulletin* (Washington, D.C.: U.S. Department of Justice, 1995), p. 7.

9. Leslie V. White, "Inside the Alcatraz of the '90s," *California Lawyer*, April 1992, pp. 44–48.

10. William Booth, "Link to the Past," *Los Angeles Times*, January 8, 1996, pp. E1, E8.

11. Douglas Dennis, "News Briefs: Jail Boom," *The Angolite*, July/August 1995, pp. 7–8.

12. Mireya Navarro, "The Inmate Gangs of Rikers Island," *The New York Times*, May 8, 1994, p. 36.

13. Ibid., pp. 29, 36.

14. David Ferrell, "A Caldron of Fear and Violence," *Los Angeles Times*, May 19, 1996, pp. A1, A14.

Chapter 4

1. Cecilia W. Dugger, "Young, Impressionable and Accused of Murder," *The New York Times*, May 17, 1994, pp. B6–7.

2. Ibid., p. E3.

3. Ronald J. Ostrow, "Number of Juvenile Murderers Is Soaring," *Los Angeles Times*, March 8, 1996, p. A18.

4. Ibid., p. A18.

5. Robert Worth, "A Model Prison," *Atlantic Monthly*, November 1995, p. 44.

6. Anne E. Weiss, *Prisons: A System in Trouble* (Hillside, N.J.: Enslow Publishers, Inc., 1988), p. 41.

7. Larry Cole, *Our Children's Keepers* (New York: Grossman Publishers, 1972), pp. xix-xxi.

8. Vernon Fox, *Introduction to Corrections*, 3rd ed. (Englewood Cliffs, N.J.: Prentice-Hall, Inc., 1985), p. 204.

9. Phyllis Elperin Clark and Robert Lehrman, *Doing Time: A Look at Crime and Prisons* (New York: Hastings House Publishers, 1980), pp. 60–61.

10. Cole, pp. xxi–xxii.

11. Ibid., pp. 3–4.

12. Ibid., pp. 5–6.

13. *Juvenile Offenders and Victims: A National Report* (Pittsburgh: National Center for Juvenile Justice, 1995), pp. 70–71.

14. Ibid., pp. 80–82.

15. Ibid., p. 82.

16. Ibid., pp. 76–79.

17. Ibid., p. 79.

18. Gwen A. Holden and Robert A. Kapler, "Deinstitutionalizing Status Offenders, A Record of Progress," *Juvenile Justice*, Fall/Winter 1995, pp. 6–7.

19. Ibid., pp. 138–139.

20. Ibid., p. 147.

21. Bill Boyarsky, "The Spin: Book Reveals Dark Side of Juvenile Justice," *Los Angeles Times*, April 7, 1996, p. B1.

22. Malcolm Braly, *False Starts: A Memoir of San Quentin and Other Prisons* (Boston: Little, Brown and Company, 1976), p. 46.

23. Joseph Bauer, "Letters From a Teenage Jail," *Seventeen*, August 1991, p. 239.

24. Ibid., p. 239.

Chapter 5

1. David Colker, "From San Quentin, a 'Dead Man' Tells His Tale," *Los Angeles Times*, April 30, 1996, p. E1.

2. *Corrections, Public Safety, Public Service* (Sacramento: California State Department of Corrections, 1993), pp. 12–15.

3. Edith Stanley, "It's a Workaday World for N. Carolina Inmates," *Los Angeles Times*, November 30, 1995, p. A5.

4. James Ricci, "Prison Weddings: Love Faces Long Odds," *Los Angeles Times*, October 18, 1996, pp. A1, A24.

5. *Drugs and Crime Facts, 1993* (Rockwell, Md.: Drugs & Crime Data Center & Clearing House, 1993), pp. 4–6.

6. Ibid., pp. 21–22.

7. Wayne S. Wooden and Jay Parker, *Men Behind Bars: Sexual Exploitation in Prison* (New York: Plenum Press, 1982), pp. 1–2.

8. Ibid., pp. 5, 18.

9. Julie Tamaki and Danica Kirka, "Despite Lock-Down at Pitchess Jail, Racial Fighting Continues," *Los Angeles Times,* January 19, 1996, p. B3.

10. Javier Rodriguez H., "Jail, Like So Much of L.A., Is a Tinderbox," *Los Angeles Times,* February 16, 1996, p. B9.

11. *48 Hours,* CBS News, Dan Rather, host, April 10, 1996.

12. Tony Lesce, *The Big House: How America's Prisons Work* (Port Townsend, Wash.: Loopmanics Unlimited, 1991), pp. 25–26.

13. Mireye Navarro, "The Inmate Gangs of Rikers Island," *The New York Times,* May 8, 1994, p. 36.

14. Lois Warburton, *Prisons* (San Diego: Lucent Books, Inc., 1993), pp. 52–53.

15. *Managing Prison Health Care and Costs* (Washington, D.C.: National Institute of Justice, 1995), p. 3.

16. Ibid., p. 3.

17. Ibid., p. 4.

18. Phyllis Elperin Clark and Robert Lehrman, *Doing Time: A Look at Crime and Prisons* (New York: Hastings House Publishers, 1980), pp. 110–112.

19. Vernon Fox, *Introduction to Corrections,* 3rd ed. (Englewood Cliffs, N.J.: Prentice-Hall, Inc., 1985), pp. 320, 328–329.

Chapter 6

1. Burk Foster, "The Meaning of Life," *The Angolite,* Angola, Louisiana State Prison, July/August 1995, p. 17.

2. Burk Foster, "When Mercy Seasons Justice," *The Angolite,* Angola, Louisiana State Prison, November/December 1995, p. 27.

3. Ibid., pp. 20–21.

4. Ibid., pp. 18–22.

5. Ibid., p. 23.

6. Juvenile Justice Clearinghouse, Rockville, Md., April 1997.

7. Mack Reed, "An Even Longer Wait on Death Row," *Los Angeles Times*, April 3, 1996, pp. A1, A14–15.

8. Tracy L. Snell, "Capital Punishment 1995," Washington, D.C.: Bureau of Justice Statistics, December 1996, pp. 1–2.

Chapter 7

1. Alan C. Miller, "'94 Prison Rolls at Record High, Study Says," *Los Angeles Times*, August 28, 1995, p. A5.

2. Mark Mauer, "Rehabilitation Reduces Recidivism," *America's Prisons: Opposing Viewpoints*, ed. David L. Bender and Bruno Leone (San Diego: Greenhaven Press, 1991), p. 33.

3. Sheryl Stolberg, "School's Out for Convicts," *Los Angeles Times*, September 14, 1995, p. A1.

4. Ibid., p. A14.

5. Ibid.

6. Gordon Dillow, "Welcome not warm at Sheriff Joe's Jail," *The Orange County Register*, April 7, 1996, pp. A1, A6.

7. Richard B. Abell, "Higher Imprisonment, Less Crime," *America's Prisons: Opposing Viewpoints*, ed. David L. Bender and Bruno Leone (San Diego: Greenhaven Press, 1991), p. 49.

8. Eugene H. Methvin, "Why Don't We Have the Prisons We Need?" *Reader's Digest*, November 1990, p. 71.

9. Ibid.

10. Christopher Baird, "Building More Prisons Will Not Solve Prison Overcrowding," *America's Prisons: Opposing Viewpoints*, ed. David L. Bender and Bruno Leone (San Diego: Greenhaven Press, 1991), pp. 121–122.

11. Charles Colson and Daniel Van Ness, "Prisons Cannot Protect Society," *America's Prisons: Opposing Viewpoints*, ed. David L. Bender and Bruno Leone (San Diego: Greenhaven Press, 1991), p. 70.

12. Lois Warburton, *Prisons* (San Diego: Lucent Books, Inc., 1993), p. 76.

13. Wilbert Rideau, "A Convict's View: 'People Don't Want Solutions,'" *Time*, August 23, 1994, p. 33.

14. Robert James Bidinotto, "Must Our Prisons Be Resorts?" *Reader's Digest*, November 1994, pp. 65–67.

15. Ibid., pp. 70–71.

16. John Irwin, "Prison Life Destroys Lives," *America's Prisons: Opposing Viewpoints*, ed. David L. Bender and Bruno Leone (San Diego: Greenhaven Press, 1991), p. 42.

17. Thomas Mathiesen, "Prisons Cannot Rehabilitate," *America's Prisons: Opposing Viewpoints*, ed. David L. Bender and Bruno Leone (San Diego: Greenhaven Press, 1991), pp. 38–43.

18. Elizabeth Mehren, "As Bad As They Wanna Be," *Los Angeles Times*, May 17, 1996, pp. E1, E3.

19. Greg Krikorian, "Flip Side of '3 Strikes' Lets Many Suspects Elude Jail," *Los Angeles Times*, August 30, 1995, pp. A1, A22.

20. Maura Dolan and Tony Perry, "Justices Deal Blow to '3 Strikes,'" *Los Angeles Times*, June 21, 1996, pp. A1, A20.

21. Stephanie Simon, "Angry 'Three Strikes' Supporters Vow to Fight Back," *Los Angeles Times*, June 21, 1996, p. A20.

22. Carla Rivera, "Study Finds Aid Outdoes 'Three Strikes' in Crime Fight," *Los Angeles Times*, June 20, 1996, p. A3.

23. Eric Schlosser, "Marijuana and the Law," *Atlantic Monthly*, September 1994, p. 85.

24. Alvin J. Bronstein, comments before the U.S. House of Representatives Subcommittee on Courts, Civil Liberties and the Administration of Justice, 1985, quoted in *America's Prisons: Opposing Viewpoints*, ed. David L. Bender and Bruno Leone (San Diego: Greenhaven Press, 1991), p. 147.

25. Michael Brennan, "A Case for Discretion," *Newsweek*, November 13, 1995, p. 18.

26. Krikorian, p. A20.

Chapter 8

1. Lois Warburton, *Prisons* (San Diego: Lucent Books, Inc., 1993), pp. 62–63.

2. Ibid., pp. 102–104.

3. Ibid., pp. 65–66.

4. Elizabeth Mehren, "Camp Crackdown," *Los Angeles Times*, June 19, 1996, p. E5.

5. Michael Gartner, "Creative Sentencing Saves Money," *America's Prisons: Opposing Viewpoints*, ed. David L. Bender and Bruno Leone (San Diego: Greenhaven Press, 1991), p. 203.

6. Steven G. Calabaresi, "Creative Sentencing Should Be Limited," *America's Prisons: Opposing Viewpoints*, ed. David L. Bender and Bruno Leone (San Diego: Greenhaven Press, 1991), pp. 209–211.

7. Gartner, p. 203.

8. Marc Mauer, "Creative Sentencing is Effective," *America's Prisons: Opposing Viewpoints*, ed. David L. Bender and Bruno Leone (San Diego: Greenhaven Press, 1991), pp. 201–212.

9. Ibid., pp. 202–203.

10. Warburton, pp. 78–79.

11. Marc Lifsher, "Private-prisons advocates may have to do time fighting guards' union," *The Orange County Register*, May 13, 1996, pp. A1, A14.

12. Ibid., p. A14.

13. Ibid.

14. Ibid., pp. A1, A14.

Glossary

alternative sentence—Sometimes called creative sentence. A community-based punishment given instead of prison.

boot camp—A type of alternative sentence that is based on strict military training, or basic training. The sentence usually has a duration of three to six months.

chain gang—A form of punishment in which inmates are chained together and taken out to work outdoors.

clemency—Forgiveness for a crime that shortens the amount of time that an inmate must stay in prison. It does not mean a full pardon.

commutation—When a prisoner serving a life sentence has his sentence reduced to a determined number of years. Also called a "time cut."

corrections officers—Prison guards.

determinate sentence—A sentence consisting of a fixed period of imprisonment.

early release—A program in which an inmate is released, usually on parole, before serving a complete sentence.

electronic monitoring—An alternative sentence in which the lawbreaker is required to wear a monitor that sends signals to a computer to check on the person's whereabouts.

felony—A conviction for a serious crime that results in a term in prison.

halfway house—A residential facility where offenders are kept in a controlled environment.

house arrest—A sentence in which the offender is required to stay in his or her own house instead of going to a prison.

incarceration—Imprisonment.

indeterminate sentence—A sentence that gives both a minimum and a maximum length of time that the offender must stay in prison. The offender is eligible for parole when the minimum sentence has been served.

jail—A local prison where offenders are held while waiting trial or waiting to go to a state or federal prison. Those who are found guilty of less serious crimes such as misdemeanors may also be kept in a jail rather than in a prison.

lethal injection—A form of execution in which a combination of deadly drugs is injected into the inmate's bloodstream.

lockup—Another term for jail.

mandatory sentence—A sentence that is required by law as a result of being convicted of certain crimes.

maximum-security prison—A prison built to house the most violent offenders. In addition to cells and walled boundaries, security is maintained by numerous armed guards and electronic security.

minimum-security prison—A prison for less violent offenders, in which inmates live in open dormitories without fences.

misdemeanor—A crime that is considered less serious than a felony.

pardon—A forgiveness for committing a crime. The prisoner is then released, and his rights and property are returned to him.

parens patriae—The doctrine that gives states the right to become involved in the lives of juvenile offenders in the place of their parents.

parole—The release of an inmate from prison, usually for good behavior, after a part of the term has been served.

penitentiary—A prison.

plea bargain—A system in which the offender is allowed to plead guilty to a lesser offense than the one he or she was arrested for. This saves the government the cost of a trial.

premeditation—Planning to commit a crime in advance.

privatization—Building and operating prisons by a private corporation that specializes in corrections.

probation—An alternative sentence that is served in the community rather than in prison.

recidivism—Returning to a life of crime after being released from prison.

rehabilitation—The belief that a prisoner's behavior can be changed so that he or she can be a productive citizen.

status offenses—Law violations committed by juveniles that would not be considered crimes if they were committed by an adult. Some examples are truancy, drinking, and running away from home.

work release—A program that allows prisoners to leave prison during the day to work or to attend school.

Further Reading

Books

Bender, David L., and Bruno Leone. *America's Prisons: Opposing Viewpoints.* San Diego: Greenhaven Press, 1991.

Clark, Phyllis Elperin, and Robert Lehrman. *Doing Time: A Look at Crime and Prison.* New York: Hastings House Publishers, 1980.

Davis, Bertha. *Instead of Prison.* New York: Franklin Watts, 1986.

Kosof, Anna. *Prison Life in America.* New York: Franklin Watts, 1984.

Loeb, Robert H., Jr. *Crime and Capital Punishment.* New York: Franklin Watts, 1986.

Owens, Lois Smith, and Vivian Verdell Gordon. *Prisons and the Criminal Justice System.* New York: Walker and Company, 1992.

Warburton, Lois. *Prisons.* San Diego: Lucent Books, Inc., 1993.

Weiss, Anne E. *Prisons: A System in Trouble.* Hillside, N.J.: Enslow Publishers, Inc., 1988.

Articles

Bidinotto, Robert James. "Must Our Prisons Be Resorts?" *Reader's Digest,* November 1994, p. 65.

———. "Revolving Door Justice: Plague on America." *Reader's Digest,* February 1994, p. 33.

Mehren, Elizabeth. "As Bad As They Wanna Be." *Los Angeles Times*, May 17, 1996, p. E1.

Methvin, Eugene. "Why Don't We Have the Prisons We Need?" *Reader's Digest*, November 1990, p. 6.

Rideau, Wilbert. "A Convict's View." *Time*, August 23, 1993, p. 3.

Stolberg, Sheryl. "School's Out for Convicts." *Los Angeles Times*, September 14, 1995, p. A1.

Van Atta, Dale. "The Scandal of Prisoner Lawsuits." *Reader's Digest*, April 1996, p. 65.

Index

125

About the Author

Marilyn Tower Oliver is a former high school teacher turned journalist and writer. She has had more than two hundred articles published in regional and national publications. Her most recent book, *Drugs: Should They Be Legalized?*, was published by Enslow Publishers in 1996.